Words of Praise f
FASTING

"What a wise and challenging exploration of one of the most misunderstood practices of the Christian life: fasting. In short, Scot McKnight explores how fasting can be a tool of ongoing conversion. I can't wait to gather a group of folks in my church, read this book together, and, with Scot McKnight's guidance, discern how we might be called not only to read about but also—more riskily!—to practice fasting."

Lauren Winner, Duke Divinity School,
author of Girl Meets God and Mudhouse Sabbath

"A very helpful work that offers a radically reorienting perspective on the Christian discipline of fasting."

Ruth Haley Barton, cofounder and president of
Transforming Center, author of Sacred Rhythms:
Arranging Our Lives for Spiritual Transformation

FASTING

scot m^cknight

THOMAS NELSON
Since 1798

NASHVILLE DALLAS MEXICO CITY RIO DE JANEIRO

Published in Nashville, Tennessee, by Thomas Nelson. Thomas Nelson is a registered trademark of Thomas Nelson, Inc.

Published in association with Greg Daniel, Daniel Literary Group, 1701 Kingsbury Dr., Suite 100, Nashville, TN 37215. www.danielliterarygroup.com.

Page Design by Casey Hooper.

Thomas Nelson, Inc., titles may be purchased in bulk for educational, business, fund-raising, or sales promotional use. For information, please e-mail SpecialMarkets@ThomasNelson.com.

All Scripture quotations are taken from the NEW REVISED STANDARD VERSION of the Bible. © 1989 by the Division of Christian Education of the National Council of the Churches of Christ in the U.S.A. All rights reserved.

ISBN 978-0-8499-4605-9 (trade paper)

Library of Congress Cataloging-in-Publication Data
McKnight, Scot.
  Fasting : fasting as body talk in the Christian tradition / Scot McKnight.
    p. cm.
  Includes bibliographical references and index.
  ISBN 978-0-8499-0108-9 (hardcover : alk. paper)
  1. Fasting—Religious aspects—Christianity. 2. Body, Human—Religious aspects—Christianity.
I. Title.
  BV5055.M35 2008
  248.4'7—dc22

                                    2008037270

Printed in the United States of America
10 11 12 13 14 RRD 6 5 4 3 2 1

For Rob and Linda Merola

CONTENTS

CONTENTS

FOREWORD

WITHIN OUR CHRISTIAN TRADITION, THERE ARE SEVEN ancient practices, or disciplines, that come to us out of Judaism and directly through the teachings and observances of the early church. Each of the seven functions as a way of incorporating our faith into our daily, human, and very physical lives. Each is, in other words, a means by which we as believers can incarnate belief and perceive it in our bodies and physical consciousness as well as in our minds.

We, as God's creatures on earth, live out our earthly lives within four dimensions—those of height, depth, breadth, and time. Of the seven ancient practices, four govern or measure time. Fixed-hour prayer incorporates daily time into the faithful life of the believer. Sabbath keeping or observance regulates and consecrates weekly time. The business of following the seasons of the liturgical year, both in our public worship and our private devotion, synchronizes the rhythms of the year for every member in the larger church universal. The making of pilgrimage, the fourth of the practices that sanctify time, is the only one of the four that has suffered much change or adjustment over the centuries. In Western Christianity, it is no longer generally seen as that once-in-a-lifetime trip, bought at great expense of time and energy for the sake of taking one's whole self to sacred or hallowed space. Rather, it is more commonly seen as a form of retreat to be entered into at less expense or difficulty than true pilgrimage, and certainly, more frequently.

The other three ancient practices have more to do with the business of living within space. They are concerned with the physical body and its awareness of itself. Of these three, fasting is far and away the most misunderstood, maligned, and misused. Tithing costs one a part of the product of one's work and a part of the substance that one has for supporting the physical and emotional needs of the body. The sacred meal, by any name, be it Eucharist or mass or Lord's Supper or Communion, brings the divine directly into the body. But fasting . . . ah, fasting. Now, there's a different matter. Fasting hurts. Fasting can become exaggerated into an excessive and neurotic indulgence. Fasting, carried too far, can harm the body . . . and fasting, submitted to theological and scriptural scrutiny, asserts that soul and body are, and that neither is without the other. For many Christians, that itself is a disturbing precept better left unexplored.

So far as I know, no one in recent (or even not-so-recent) years has taken on fasting with the deftness and clarity that theologian Scot McKnight exercises here. McKnight's own Christian faith shows on every page of this book, as does his vast scholarship. But what shows most, I think, is his pastoral concern that the church come again to a time when we understand and embrace the spiritual benefits and religious necessity of fasting—

to a time when we can accept it not just as an antique exercise once practiced by our forebears, but as one our Lord himself both followed and taught as necessary at certain times.

This is, in sum, not a book for the cowardly. Instead, it is a book for the courageous Christian who seeks to more fully occupy all the member parts of his or her own life, and to do so for the expressed purposes of better knowing and serving God.

Phyllis Tickle
General Editor
Ancient Practices Series

INTRODUCTION: A MONTAGE OF CHRISTIAN VOICES ON FASTING

FASTING IS A PERSON'S WHOLE-BODY, NATURAL RESPONSE to life's sacred moments. Because fasting is natural, it is found in all the great world religions and philosophies. Unfortunately, fasting is the most misunderstood of the Christian spiritual disciplines. We will discuss the reasons for this opening salvo later, but for now I'd like to offer a montage, a splicing together of statements about fasting from the days of King David until now.

KING DAVID: FASTING AS A WHOLE-BODY ACT

In the middle of the Old Testament, what Jews call the Tanakh or the Hebrew Bible, is a collection of Israel's favorite prayers. We learn so many things in the Psalms, not the least of which is that prayer has a bundle of natural companions—like prayer and kneeling, prayer and pleading, prayer and pondering, prayer and struggling, and prayer and praising.

One of prayer's companions is fasting. Here are four lines from the middle of the thirty-fifth psalm. David tells us all that when his enemies were "sick," he didn't gloat. Instead, he got to work praying for them:

> But as for me, when they were sick,
>> I wore sackcloth;
>> I afflicted myself with *fasting*.
> I prayed with head bowed on my bosom,
>> as though I grieved for a friend or a brother;
> I went about as one who laments for a mother,
>> bowed down and in mourning. (Ps. 35:13–14, emphasis added)

In this psalm, David is not being overly dramatic or trying to get us to see how righteous he was or how wicked his opponents were. His prayer was accompanied by fasting. For David, as for everyone in the Bible, prayer was *whole-body* activity, the way some Christians raise their hands in worship or kneel on kneelers during confession time. My favorite writer about the Psalms, John Goldingay, tells us that David's sadness was not yet fully bloomed until the body—in this case, fasting—was involved: "The psalm assumes that merely to feel sadness is not enough; because we are physical creatures and not just minds and spirits, it would be odd not to express sorrow in (e.g.) abstention from food and then afflicting one's spirit and one's self."[1]

Skip ahead a few centuries to the prophet Isaiah.

ISAIAH: FASTING AS AN ACT FOR OTHERS

Fasting, like other spiritual practices, easily drifted into self-righteousness and self-absorption among ancient Israelites. If fasting did not lead to compassion for others, God revealed through the prophet Isaiah, then it was falling apart before it did its work. Isaiah made his point by asking his audience a series of questions:

> Is not this the fast that I choose:
>> to loose the bonds of injustice,
>>> to undo the thongs of the yoke,
>> to let the oppressed go free,
>>> and to break every yoke?

> Is it not to share your bread with the hungry,
>> and bring the homeless poor into your house;
> when you see the naked, to cover them,
>> and not to hide yourself from your own kin? (Isa. 58:6–7)

These words must remain at the center of all teaching about fasting. Every generation needs an Isaiah to stand up in the middle of the action and say, "Hey, folks, this isn't about us! What we give up when we fast should be given to others."

Skip ahead nearly a millennium.

EARLY CHRISTIAN FATHERS: FASTING AS
A SACRED RHYTHM AND A DISCIPLINE

St. Athanasius, one of the architects of Christian orthodoxy and a deeply pious saint, knew the formative powers of the sacred rhythms of the church calendar. That calendar weaved in and out of mourning over sin (fasting) and celebrating the good grace of God (feasting). "Sometimes," he says of the church calendar, "the call is made to fasting, and sometimes to a feast."[2]

St. Athanasius's near contemporary, St. Augustine, took fasting into another area of formation. One way for Christians to find victory over temptation, St. Augustine reminded his readers, was to fast. Why? "Because it is sometimes necessary to check the delight of the flesh in respect to licit pleasures in order to keep it from yielding to illicit joys."[3]

These two themes—fasting as a sacred rhythm in the church calendar and fasting as discipline against sinful desires—are perhaps the most important themes of fasting in the history of Christian thinking. Skip ahead now more than another millennium.

JOHN CALVIN AND ANDREW MURRAY:
FASTING AS INNER RESOLUTION

John Calvin's *Institutes of the Christian Religion* formed the theology and spirituality of the Reformed wing of the Christian church. Ever keen to focus on piety and prevent distractions of any kind, Calvin wrote about the significance of fasting when it came to serious concerns in prayer. Thus, he says, "whenever men are to pray to God concerning any great matter, it would be expedient to appoint fasting along with prayer. Their sole purpose in this kind of fasting is to render themselves more eager and unencumbered for prayer . . . with a full stomach our mind is not so lifted up to God."[4]

Andrew Murray, a prominent Reformed minister in Cape Town, South Africa, well known for the spreading influence of his warmhearted evangelical piety, said this about fasting: "Fasting helps us to express, to deepen, and to confirm the resolution that we are ready to sacrifice anything, even ourselves, to attain the Kingdom of God."[5]

Fasting as a demonstration before God of our inner resolution and yearning has also shaped how we understand fasting.

ADALBERT DE VOGÜÉ:
DELIGHT IN THE DISCIPLINE

St. Benedict, the great preacher from Norcia, Italy, included fasting when he formulated his classic *Rule*. The monastic tradition that derives from him has also shaped how many understand fasting today. My favorite expression of fasting in the Roman Catholic monastic tradition comes from Adalbert de

Vogüé, a Benedictine monk who has rigorously fasted for decades. His book jars many with the words of its title: *To Love Fasting*. What de Vogüé learned as he disciplined his body in fasting can be a lesson for all of us. "Fasting was no longer a constraint and penance for me, but a joy and need of body and soul. I practiced it spontaneously because I loved it."[6]

Fasting has become a bit trendy in the last few years, and so I turn now to a brief selection of a few recent statements about fasting.

RECENT REMINDERS ABOUT FASTING

Perhaps no one has brought the church back to the sense of fasting as whole-body activity the way Dallas Willard has. This professor in philosophy and profound writer on the spiritual disciplines speaks of fasting in ways that lead us straight back to King David and the Bible: "But the new life in Christ simply is not an inner life of belief and imagination, even if spiritually inspired. It is a life of the whole embodied person in the social context."[7]

Along the same line as that mapped by Willard, John Piper, a Baptist pastor, fashions the Christian understanding of fasting as whole-body hungering for God. The saints of the church were fasters, Piper points out. He writes, "They were hungry enough for God's leading that they wanted to say it with the hunger of their bodies and not just the hunger of their hearts."[8]

Fasting is not only delightful, but it can liberate us at the deepest level and in life-transforming ways. Thomas Ryan, a Roman Catholic priest, reminds us that fasting taps into God's grace. In his book *The Sacred Art of Fasting*, Ryan writes, "The tendency is to think that God will love us if we change, but God loves us so that we *can* change. Penitential practices and disciplines [like fasting] enable us to appropriate and make real in our lives the freedom given through grace."[9]

No one puts this montage together better than Amy Johnson Frykholm. "Fasting," she concludes, "is about three things: attentiveness, compassion and freedom."[10]

A ➔ B ➔ C

With so many witnesses before us, is there anything left to be said?

I think there is. Allow me to lay my cards on the table right now by offering a definition of fasting and then explaining why it is the most misunderstood of the Christian spiritual disciplines.

Fasting is the natural, inevitable response of a person to a grievous sacred moment in life.

I believe fasting is *natural*. Choosing not to eat or drink is how a person naturally responds to a grievous sacred moment. Furthermore, I also believe fasting is *inevitable* if we encounter a certain kind of sacred moment. Next, and perhaps most important in our definition, I believe fasting is a *response to a serious, or grievous, sacred moment*. As we will show in the chapter that follows, people fasted in the Bible *in response* to some grievous event in life—like death or the realization of sin or when the nation was threatened.

Fasting, then, is a natural, inevitable response of a person to a grievous sacred moment. Does it bring results? Yes, but that's not the point of fasting. Those who fasted in response to grievous sacred moments frequently—*but not always!*—received results, like answered prayer. But focusing on the results causes us to misunderstand fasting entirely.

Which leads us now to see fasting in an A ➜ B ➜ C framework. If one wants to see the full Christian understanding of fasting, one must begin with A, the grievous sacred moment. That sacred moment generates a response (B), in this case fasting. Only then, only when the sacred moment is given its full power does the response of fasting generate the results (C)—and then not always, if truth be told.

What we are getting at here is very important: *fasting isn't a manipulative tool that guarantees results.* Here is something I have believed for a long, long time but that I have not heard enough in Christian discussion about fasting. The focus in our deepest Christian tradition is not moving from column B to column C but the A ➜ B movement. Fasting is a *response* to a sacred moment, not an instrument designed to get desired results. The focus in the Christian tradition is not "if you fast you will *get*," but "when *this* happens, God's people fast." Fasting is a response to a very serious situation, not an act that gets us from a good level to a better level. To make this more graphic, here's a table with a sample of possibilities:

A	B	C
Sacred Moment	**Fasting**	**Results**
Death		Life
Sin		Forgiveness
Fear	Responsive Fasting	Safety
Threats		Hope
Needs		Answers
Sickness		Health

Many today discover that they need something in the C column. They reason that since the saints got results when they fasted, they, too, will fast so they can get what they want. In other words, *the intent* of such persons is to fast *in order to* bring about a desired reward or result. Fasting for such persons is "instrumental"—it is the instrument we pull out when we are in desperate need. Every now and then fasting like this "works," and measurable results lead someone to stand up in a room, waving a hanky, to tell everyone that if we fasted more, we'd get more results. Thus, the theory is this: *fasting produces results.*

My own study of what the Bible says about fasting proves

something contrary to this instrumental approach to fasting. Namely, instead of the instrumental view of fasting, the Bible presents a *responsive* view of fasting. Fasting is a response to a grievous sacred moment. Turned around, those who are most moved by sacred moments find themselves fasting and, *because they are in tune with what God is doing in this world in those grievous sacred moments*, they may discover desired results. But such persons did not fast to get results; they fasted *in response* to sacred moments. They were in B because of the grievous sacredness of A. They didn't do B in order to make C happen.

I have come to this conclusion about fasting: when the grievous sacred moment is neglected and instead we focus on the results, fasting becomes a manipulative device instead of a genuine, Christian spiritual discipline. Far too much of the conversation today about fasting is about what we can get and not enough about the serious and severe sacred moments that prompt fasting.

This deep Christian tradition is all about the process of moving from A to B, the response of Christians to life's grievous or serious sacred moments, and not the movement from column B to C, the desire for some tangible reward.

But this definition of the biblical view of fasting assumes something that forms the biggest problem for fasting today: our definition assumes we are united in body and soul. Thus, we turn now to what we found earlier with King David and Dallas Willard: fasting is a whole-body action. Fasting as whole-body action is rooted in what I will call *body image*. I believe fasting is the most misunderstood of the spiritual practices, because the ancient wisdom that connected the body to the spirit has been either lost or distorted through dualism.

1

FASTING AND
BODY IMAGE

CHRISTIANITY HAS PERENNIALLY HAD A PROBLEM WITH
the human body.

At times in the history of the church, Christians have viewed
desires and the body as the enemy. In the past few years, the
question seems to have been, "What's the body got to do with
spirituality?" Yet we are finding today a surging interest in what
can only be called *embodied spirituality*. Young Christians express
worship with their hands aloft and their eyes closed, more and
more find spiritual strength in candles and icons, and some
churches are bringing back kneelers. Other churches encourage
releasing creative gifts for acting, painting, and art. Fasting, too,
is on the rise.

What is this all about? Thomas Howard, an evangelical
who first converted to Anglicanism and then to Catholicism,
gets it right with these words: "We are all sacramentalists

whether our theology admits it or not: we like physical contact with history."[1] Indeed, there is a rise—let's call it what it really is, a revival—of the value of embodied spirituality. We worship God and we love God *in our bodies and with our bodies and in concrete, physical, tangible, palpable ways.* Deep in the yearning of humans is the need to "do spirituality" with the body.

This raises a problem for fasting. Fasting is whole-body stuff. Many of us are much more comfortable with candles and icons and kneelers than we are with throwing our bodies into this business of worship and prayer. When it comes down to it, this revival of embodied spirituality has one major territory to conquer for Westerners. We've got a body problem. In the next chapter, I aim to reconnect the spirituality of fasting with the body. *Body talk,* my expression for what fasting is designed to be, flows out of our body image. Until we have a healthier body image, an image of the body united with the spirit, it is not likely that body talk (fasting) will occur as it should.

So, once again, the aim of this book is to reconnect body and soul (or spirit) so that fasting becomes natural and inevitable when you and I encounter a grievous sacred moment that summons us to fast. These kinds of sacred moments confront us annually, but we often don't respond to them with fasting because that practice has become so unnatural. Why? Because many of us don't see a connection between spirituality and body. Even for the increasing number of people who do see the connection—or at least who want to make that connection—acclimating the body to fasting as a natural response to sacred moments takes time. Since fasting flows out of the natural connection of body and soul, we will do well to look briefly at various body images at work in our Western culture. We begin with the Bible's wondrous emphasis on our organic unity.

BIBLICAL BODY IMAGE: ORGANIC UNITY

What strikes a reader today is how significant the body is in the Bible. The ancient Israelites and early Christians "did spirituality" in the body and with the body. What strikes observers of the church is how insignificant the body has become, though there is evidence of a yearning for a more embodied spirituality. Let's take a quick look at what the Bible says and clarify what we need to see is this: *in the Bible, humans are organic unities.*

The Bible uses a bursting bundle of specific terms for humans, and these terms overlap with one another.[2] The singular contribution of the ancient Israelites to understanding humans is found in Genesis 1:27:

> So God created humankind in his *image,*
>> in the *image* of God he created them;
>> male and female he created them. (emphasis added)

Humans, this text tells us, are "images" (I prefer the Greek word, *Eikon)* of God. As God's Eikons, we represent God on earth and govern this world for God. In addition, we engage in relationships with God, self, others, and the entire world. These roles of governing and relating are what it means to be an Eikon. And we do what God has called us to do in this world in a physical body. Like a diamond, an embodied Eikon is a multi-faceted *organic unity* of heart and mind and soul and spirit and body. As a diamond refracts light only when all the sides are working, so we need every dimension of who we are to be at work. But we have minimized the body so much in our spirituality that fasting has become unnatural.

There are many "faces," or terms for the Eikon, in the Bible. Each of these terms is important, but it is even more important to understand their organic unity. We begin with the Hebrew Bible (Old Testament), where we find the following terms describing the various dimensions of our organic unity:

soul (*nepesh*)
flesh (*basar*)
spirit (*ruach*)
heart (*leb*)

In the New Testament, we find:

heart (*kardia*)
soul (*psyche*)

flesh (*sarx*)

body (*soma*)

mind (*nous*)

spirit (*pneuma*)

will (*thelema*)

Let it be said again: in the Bible, all these terms work together to form an organic unity. The Eikon is composed of these things, but the Eikon is a unified person. What has happened is that we have cut the multifaceted diamond into two parts, the good part and the not-so-good part, assigning the various terms for the Eikon to one of two parts. The two parts are "body" and "soul/spirit." The body is the not-so-good part, and the soul is the good, eternal part. Dividing the Eikon, or person, into two parts is what makes fasting so difficult today. Since fasting is a very physical thing, it must be assigned to the body. And since fasting concerns only the body, it can't be that important, we think. Here's what the two parts look like:

Body	Soul/Spirit
Body	Soul
Flesh	Spirit
Heart	Mind
Earthly life	Will
Fasting	Eternal life
	No fasting

If fasting is the natural response of a unified person to a sacred moment, then the moment we relegate bodies to the unimportant part of our existence we also cease to see the value of fasting. If we want to discover the deepest dimensions of the Christian tradition of fasting, we will have to reconnect the "body" column with the "soul/spirit" column. When that happens, we will encounter a sacred moment, and *we will fast naturally.*

Unfortunately, we have some work to do, and much of it has to do with recapturing a healthy body image. We have to do this work because dualism has worked like yeast into every-thing we do.

BODY IMAGES TODAY

You and I have inherited the church's problem with the body whether we like it or not—whether we are Christians or not. It's part of our Western DNA. Those of us with a Western mind-set have consistently struggled to embrace the indissoluble unity of humans—body and soul/spirit—at the forefront of spirituality. To repeat what was said a moment ago, we cut ourselves up into soul and body. The soul is immortal and the body mortal. Therefore, the body doesn't ultimately (or eternally) matter.

Wired with this Western mind-set, our bodies and our spirits don't work together very well. As I think of how we look at our body image today, four common images come to mind. We see the body

- as a monster to be conquered;
- as a celebrity to be glorified;
- as a cornucopia to be filled;
- as a wallflower to be ignored.

Each of these body images shapes whether or not we fast and, if we do, how and why we fast.

Which of these—and we could easily add more—is your body image? I'll tell you where I fit when I finish this caricature.

A MONSTER TO BE CONQUERED

Some see the body as a *monster of desires* that needs to be tamed by imposing spirit over the body to conquer these unwanted desires. These folks are *ascetics*. For those who have a body-as-monster body image, fasting attempts to control the desires of the body. Some with this view become radical ascetics intent on keeping desires suppressed. People with this body image are often dedicated to purity or holiness or service, and they focus their spirituality on the kingdom to come, on heaven. Some with this view of the body have become saints; some starved themselves to death. (I'll avoid mentioning names.)

A CELEBRITY TO BE GLORIFIED

Others see the body as a *celebrity* that needs to be glorified. Such a body image makes a person a modern *narcissist*. Such persons are dedicated to happiness, individualism, and personal freedom. They are also dedicated to a slender body, tight buns, fashionable clothing, trendy haircuts, and sleek glasses, and are always in need of a mirror. Fasting for these folks is secularized—that is, it morphs into dieting for the sake of self-preservation and attractiveness. Some in this crowd have also become canonized saints; many more have glorified themselves into a life not well spent.

A CORNUCOPIA TO BE FILLED

Some see the body as a *cornucopia*, the twisting horn that is filled with an endless supply of rich and sumptuous fruits and fancy foods. Those who see the body as a cornucopia are modern *hedonists* and have no use for fasting. They are dedicated to physical pleasure, rich diets, delicate palates, expensive drinks, and special restaurants. They love food, what Frederica Mathewes-Green calls that "intoxicating pleasure" and our little "cute sin."[3] These folks push their hearts into their bellies. Their spirituality derives from health and wealth and pleasures. Hedonists consider those who fast killjoys or radical ascetics. They might even accuse those who fast of trying to earn their way to heaven. Some in this crowd have become saints; some have eaten themselves to death.

A WALLFLOWER TO BE IGNORED

Others see the body as a *wallflower* that can be ignored because it doesn't matter. Fasting is little more than a strange custom practiced by a foreign spirituality. These folks are *neo-Gnostics*, for whom the body is a shell and for whom only the insides—the spirit or the soul or especially the mind—really matter. Those who see the body as a wallflower are dedicated to spirituality, meditation on the Bible, contemplative experience, and speculative thinking—even out-of-body mystical experiences. They focus on the kingdom above, beyond, and outside the body and real world. Some in this crowd have become saints; most have missed the intensity of a full-bodied commitment to following Jesus.

FASTING AS BODY TALK

Ascetics encounter grievous sacred moments, indwell them, and may never get out of them. Celebrities encounter grievous sacred moments and pretend they did not happen. Hedonists encounter grievous sacred moments and turn the other way. Neo-Gnostics encounter grievous sacred moments and say they are "this-worldly" and need not concern them.

But this book's emphasis is on fasting as *body talk*, because a body image of organic unity is what we need most if we seek to develop a fully integrated spiritual life that includes fasting. Pope John Paul II was the twentieth century's most charismatic

Christian leader, but he was also a profound theologian. The pinnacle of his theological leadership can be found in his brilliant *Man and Woman He Created Them.*[4] John Paul II essentially argued that our bodies reflect the giving and receiving life of the Trinity. Our bodies and what we do with our bodies visibly demonstrate the very core of what we are made to do: love God and love others.[5] For those with a healthy body image of an organic unity, fasting is a natural and inevitable response to life's grievous, or serious, sacred moments. I think the former pope's book, though it is not about fasting, is one of the most important books for those who want to understand what a Christian body image is all about.

I foolishly stated at the top of this section that I'd admit my own view, but first let me ask you this question: which are you? Now that you've answered, I'll answer too. I think of my body as a wallflower but tend to act as if it's a cornucopia, which means I'm overweight and don't care enough about it to do something radical, such as making a major lifestyle change. The only time I ever thought of my body as a celebrity was when I was in high school, still dreaming of a professional sports career and therefore caught up in typical teenage vanity about how talented and good-looking I was (or thought I was). Now I don't think about my body all that much and so I pretend it is a wallflower, but like a cornucopia, it rarely runs on empty. So I need this book as much as anyone else, and perhaps more.

What we think of our bodies matters, so maybe you should

take a good look in the mirror and in your heart and ask yourself what kind of body image you have. Your body image opens a window into your spirituality.

The thesis of this work is simple: a unified perception of body, soul, spirit, and mind creates a spirituality that includes the body. For this kind of body image, fasting is natural. Fasting is the body talking what the spirit yearns, what the soul longs for, and what the mind knows to be true. It is body talk—not the body simply talking for the spirit, for the mind, or for the soul in some symbolic way, but for the person, the whole person, to express herself or himself completely. Fasting is one way you and I bring our entire selves into complete expression. The Bible, because it advocates clearly that the person—heart, soul, mind, spirit, body—is embodied as a unity, assumes that fasting as body talk is inevitable.

The emphasis of fasting as body talk operates with another theory: until we embrace a more unified sense of the body, it is unlikely that fasting will return as a routine response to grievous sacred moments. Many today complain that Christians no longer fast; the warnings emerge from the voices of Roman Catholics as well as evangelical Protestants. Here are stereotypical words one can read or hear: "The Bible teaches fasting, and church tradition teaches fasting; therefore, Christians should return to the practice of fasting. It's the original and ancient way of spirituality." So says the voice of complaint.

I don't believe the problem is the willpower of God's people.

The problem is body image. Urging folks today to fast is like urging them to milk their own cows—just as there are no cows in their backyards, so there is no body in their perception of spirituality. Western DNA and fasting are connected by the slenderest of threads. The urge to fast will not return among Christians until we understand the connection of body and soul. When that happens, we will once again discover the A ➜ B ➜ C pattern: sacred moment, response in fasting, and results. As Kathleen Dugan stated, "Fasting in Christianity is only truly itself when it realizes the sacredness of the body."[6]

A reader informed me recently that he and his wife gave up drinking anything but water during Lent. When I told some of my students at North Park University about this family's practice during Lent, the typical response was this: "What for?" The befuddlement in the students' question is why urging Christians to fast today requires a new kind of patience. Fasting, frankly, doesn't make sense to most of us until we have grasped the importance of the body for our spirituality.

PART 1

SPIRITUALITY AND FASTING

2

FASTING AS
BODY TALK

IN THE EARLY DAYS OF RESEARCHING AND WRITING THIS
book, I daily interrupted my work for lunch. One time I turned
off the computer for a plenteous luncheon with some church
leaders from Indianapolis at Trattoria Pomigliano, my favorite
local Italian restaurant. Normally, however, I simply stopped
for a lunch by myself at home. When chomping into my daily
turkey sandwich, I sensed the oddity of thinking about fasting
while eating. I know this: *all* people think about eating while
they are fasting because hunger pains are present. But, I pon-
dered to myself, fewer think about fasting while eating. So I
decided that my routine "hypocrisy" of eating while writing
about fasting had to end. About a third of the way through this
book, I began to skip my lunches—which made me think about
food more than I normally do—but it gave me the tactile experience of what I was writing. Writing a book, I believe, is a serious—if not also grievous at times—endeavor, and focusing on

that seriousness enabled me to convert the process of writing this book into a sacred moment worthy of fasting.

The oddity of my experience illustrates the point of this chapter: what I thought and believed to be important was not what my body was doing. This is not a simple case of hypocrisy, for I wasn't fooling myself or anyone else. I was being a dualist at some level. I was telling myself, in my mind, that fasting was important and that my book was a serious endeavor, but my body was not engaged. It was good enough for me at that time to *think* about fasting and even to *believe* in it—it was good enough to have my *spirit* say that fasting was good. But a mental agreement wasn't enough. I sensed a need to make my writing enough of a sacred moment that it prompted a whole-body act. So I started fasting on days I wrote this book. It brought my body and spirit back together.

In this chapter, I will explore the unity of the person in Christian thinking because it shapes what we do when it comes to fasting. Most of us know that Christians, unlike Platonists and Gnostics, believe the person is a unity—body and soul and spirit and mind together form the person. We know this, or at least we say we do. But our Western mind-set does everything it can to break down the unity of the person, to separate body from spirit and soul. In a world more influenced by the impact of Plato on such writers as Immanuel Kant, Sigmund Freud, and Charles Darwin, we need to remind ourselves again of the organic unity of humans and how this reshapes the meaning of fasting.[1]

ORGANIC UNITY AND OUR DEFINITION OF FASTING

As noted in chapter 1, humans are made as God's Eikons. A variety of terms can be used to describe humans in their various facets, terms like *soul* and *spirit* and *body* and *heart*. But no matter which term we use, you and I are organic unities, and we cannot lose sight of that unity.

There is, however, a reason that dualism develops. Each person, however you divide up the terms in the previous chapter, is both an *outer* physical person and an *inner* spiritual person. The Bible does not say the body *contains* a spirit, like a beaker into which we pour a liquid, but that each person *is* a spirit and *is* body. In other words, the Christian tradition teaches that there is a *duality* about humans, but there is not a *dualism*. We are one person with an inner and outer dimension, but we are not comprised of two parts—an inner part and an outer part. Neither is it right to think that one is good (the inner) and the other bad (the outer).[2] Understanding the difference between our duality is very important for fasting.

The problem for fasting is that, for centuries, Christians have had a tendency to let our duality slide into a dualism—with the inner or spiritual realm overwhelming the outer, bodily person. Can we find a middle way? Can the Eikon be restored to an organic unity within itself? I believe so. Biblical fasting is about joining the material to the immaterial, the body to the soul, the body to the spirit in a unified, organic act. (The terms *soul* and *spirit* in the Christian tradition are not always easy to distinguish, so I use them interchangeably here.) Fasting in accordance with the Bible occurs when the whole person—the embodied spirit or the "inspirited" body—fasts. Lynne Baab got this right in her study of the biblical view of fasting when it comes to expressing grief:

> When we are deeply absorbed in grief, habitual activities and normal pleasures feel inappropriate and out of place. We want to shout, "Stop the world! The one I loved is no longer alive, and I can't bear it!" That desire to stop everything normal, to let ourselves be absorbed by our loss and pain, is manifested by stopping our consumption of food.[3]

Fasting is the expression of the whole person, and when the whole person is united within itself, fasting is natural.

Before we continue, remember our definition of fasting. *Fasting is the natural, inevitable response of a person to a grievous sacred moment in life.* Now let's put some flesh and bones on the word *fasting*. Fasting is choosing not to indulge in food and sustenance. The biblical sense of fasting normally involved not eating anything from sunup to sundown (twelve hours) or perhaps from sundown to sundown (twenty-four hours). Absolute fasts involve denying the body food and water. Rarely does a fast in the Bible extend beyond twelve hours, though sometimes it does.

To say that fasting means "not to indulge" opens up the door for some creative ideas. Some today use the word *fasting* for not watching TV during Lent, abstaining from desserts, or not watching sports on Sunday. Each of these can be a good discipline for specific individuals, but I do not believe it is accurate to call these things *fasting*. Why? Because fasting in the Bible describes *not eating or not drinking*. In the Bible, fasting is about not eating food or (rarely) about not drinking water. To choose not to watch TV or not to eat savory meats on Friday is not fasting but abstinence. I think it is important to distinguish between fasting and abstinence, and I will do so throughout this book. Some differ with me here; I ask only to be permitted to use the terms as I judge the evidence.

Fasting is a choice not to eat for a designated period because some moment is so sacred that partaking in food would deface or profane the seriousness of the moment. When Israel sinned and called for a fast connected to repentance, eating would have shattered the seriousness of the repentance. They felt it necessary that the body be afflicted to express their repentance. When Israel summoned others to fast in order to plead with God to protect the nation from war, eating would have profaned the sacred respect for the nation. When Israel grieved over death, any kind of physical comfort or pleasure would have broken the somber nature of their grief.

I believe biblical fasting begins right here: because of the sacredness of some moment or a task ahead, an embodied person chooses to avoid physical indulgence for a period of time in order to focus attention on God. Fasting, to return to our A ➜ B ➜ C pattern, is a response to a sacred moment. One fasts because it seems a sacrilege to eat in this sacred moment. What I am impressed with as I read the Bible is how rarely the C element (results) even comes up. What is very important to realize is that C is never the motivation for B. The motivation for B (fasting) is always A (the sacred moment).

I want to explore the responsive nature of fasting in one more way. At the very core of fasting is empathy with the divine or participation in God's perception of a sacred moment. When someone dies, God is grieved; when someone sins, particularly egregiously, God is grieved; when a nation is threatened, God is grieved. We could provide more examples. The point is this: fasting identifies with God's perspective and grief in a sacred moment. Fasting enables us to identify with how God views a given event; fasting empowers us to empathize with God. Fasting is about *pathos*, taking on the emotions of God in a given event. This will be explored at times in what follows, but for now I use it to illustrate the very important point that fasting is a *response* to a sacred moment and not an *instrument* to get what we want. When people tell us they are fasting, we should ask, "In response to what?" instead of, "What do you hope you will get out of it?"

KINDS OF FASTING

One area of confusion I hear when people speak of fasting is the various kinds of fasting. It might be helpful if we list the kinds of fasting we find both in the Bible and in the Christian tradition of fasting.

FASTING

I begin with normal fasting, which is sometimes called a *water fast*. In normal fasting, a person consumes only water for a specific period of time. Because a lengthy water fast makes extreme demands upon the body, some suggest instead a *juice fast*. In a juice fast, the person consumes only juices—which have more nutrients than water—for a specified period. There are significant differences between water and juice fasting, but for now those distinctions can be left to the side. Liquid fasting is how the Bible portrays the normal kind of fasting, which is the choice not to consume food or sustenance for a given time period.

ABSTINENCE

In addition to the liquid fasts, there is the *partial food fast*. Because the prophet Daniel abstained from specific kinds of foods, some call this the *Daniel fast*. Whatever one calls it, some abstain from delicacies or a particular food (chocolate, red meat, pasta, caffeine) for a specific period of time as a form of disciplining the body. Some abstain from all foods except vegetables while others abstain from everything but dry foods and grains. The fourth-century desert fathers and mothers were known for this. In the Eastern Orthodox churches, fasting sometimes involves abstaining from meats, fish, dairy products, eggs, oil, and alcohol. Partial food fasting would be better termed *abstinence*. As mentioned previously, abstinence is to be distinguished from fasting, which is the choice not to eat any food or sustenance for a prescribed period.

ABSOLUTE FASTING

The most radical fast of all is the *absolute* fast, during which a person neither eats nor drinks anything for a specific period. Chapter 13 discusses the health dangers to fasting, so I urge you at this point to consider reading that chapter should you be tempted to jump into absolute fasting.

What kind of fasting did the ancient Israelites and early Christians practice? We can't be sure—the Bible doesn't give us a manual on fasting. What seems most likely is that they fasted from evening dinner until either midday the next day or until dinner the next day. It is possible they fasted after breakfast until dinner that evening, but it seems more likely that the term *fast* described not eating from one evening meal until the next evening meal.

A WARNING: NO SIMPLE PROMISES

It is not unusual to find great stories about the sanctity and success of Christians who routinely fast. In fact, there appears to be a cottage industry of connecting great Christians with fasting, then suggesting that great Christians fast, and then suggesting that fasting is necessary to be a great Christian or that it was fasting that made them noble. Alongside this logical fallacy is another: prayer warriors fast, and it is the fasting that makes their warring in prayer with God so effective. I do not dispute that many great Christians have fasted or that many prayer warriors have fasted. What I do dispute is that it is the fasting that made them great Christians and effective in prayer.

This approach to fasting, which probably every preacher or writer on fasting is tempted to copy or use in a sermon, gets our A → B → C pattern mixed up. Yes, sometimes fasters achieve great results, but the results were not their primary motivation. Instead, there was a yearning out of a grievous sacred moment that naturally found expression in fasting. That yearning is what led to the results, not the fasting. But, again, the temptation is to show how great fasting can be by talking about the impact of great saints who fasted.

As we turn now to discuss how the Bible and the Christian tradition talk about fasting, I will avoid offering great examples of those who might illustrate my point—and I do this to avoid suggesting that those who fast are successful. I'm hoping that our approach to fasting as a response to grievous sacred moment might trigger a connection between spirit and body. I'm praying that this connection will create in us a unified person who responds to life's sacred moments by fasting naturally.

3

FASTING AS
BODY TURNING

PERHAPS THE MOST COMMON FORM OF FASTING IN THE
Bible will surprise us. The most common form of fasting is in
response to the kind of sacred moment when Israel is called to
confess sin. I call this kind of fasting *body turning*. One of the
more picturesque words in the Hebrew Bible, what most
Christians call the Old Testament, is the word *repent*. This
English word translates the Hebrew word *shuv*, which means to
turn around. Hence, fasting in connection with repentance is
body turning. When transferred into a metaphor, we can say
that repentance involves "turning around" morally. We sometimes say one "turns over a new leaf" or "turns the tide" or
"turns tail" or "turns the corner"—and each of these phrases
evokes what the Hebrew *shuv* evoked.

Because Israel's perception of the person was unified,
repentance often expressed itself in the physical act of fasting.

The moment of turning from sin and back to God, of turning from a false path onto the path of light, of empathizing with God's grief over Israel's sin, was so sacred and so filled with the potential of the grace-giving God that Israelites chose not to eat.

The odd thing about the modern church is that the sacred moment of repentance, which is a very serious moment, rarely leads to fasting. Think of our conversions and baptisms, the pre-eminent moments of repentance, and ask this: is there a more appropriate place than our conversion process for a time of repentance by way of fasting? Is there a need for a place in our church calendar—not just universal but also local—for repentance as a group by fasting? We celebrate at times with potlucks and barbecues and banquets, but do we ever "de-celebrate" and repent by gathering together to fast? Is there a need for more of us to deal with sins both private and personal by empathizing with God's grief over our own sins by fasting? I think so. Perhaps we need to ponder these things more in order to lead us not only to the God of grace but also to a more dignified and unified sense of the body and spirit. Is there not a need for body turning for all of us?

This is theory. What about the practice of a fast of repentance as we find it in the Bible? When should we engage our entire person in a fast of repentance, in body turning? Here are four suggestions that flow straight out of the wisdom we find in the Bible.

DURING LENT AND HOLY WEEK

God drew up a calendar for Israel and gave his people some things to remember every year, just as we Americans remember the Fourth of July and Christmas and Easter and the birthdays of our heroes. Our national and personal histories are kept alive by memory, so God instructed Israel to remember some major events. One of Israel's annual memorials was devoted entirely to the public and personal confession of sin; in other words, it was a day to repent. Every year, all of Israel gathered together in Jerusalem to do one thing: repent from last year's sins.

That day was called Yom Kippur, or the Day of Atonement. On the tenth day of the seventh month, Moses says, the children of Israel were to celebrate the "day of atonement" (Lev. 23:27). Several things happened on the annual Day of Atonement: Israel confessed sin, God covered the sins of Israel (*covered* is a translation for *atoned*), the temple was purified, and Israel and God were again reconciled.

Integral to Israel's confession was fasting, or body turning. On that day, Leviticus 23:27 says, Moses told Israel, "Deny yourselves." And so serious was this denial of self that God warned, "anyone who does not practice self-denial during that entire day shall be cut off from the people [excommunicated]" (v. 29). That's what you call serious. Anyone who labored on that day was to be destroyed (v. 30). That's even more serious.

Because ancient Israel began the day at sunset, the Bible says this discipline of self-denial was to last from "evening to evening (v. 32)." We sometimes label the Day of Atonement an *absolute* fast—no food or water for twenty-four hours.

Behind the English "deny yourselves" in Leviticus 23:27 is the Hebrew word *'anah,* which means "to afflict oneself" or "to afflict one's throat." Nearly all experts agree that the self-denial involved here was at least to deny oneself of food and probably also water. Most also think this self-denial involved more extreme measures—like sleeping on the floor, refusing friendship, refraining from washing oneself or anointing oneself, and probably also abstaining from sexual intercourse. Put together, the Israelites were told to make their life uncomfortable for an entire day in order to bring their entire person into harmony with the gravity of sin and the need to turn from sin toward God. God thought this was so important that Israel was summoned to enact the Day of Atonement every year.

The three elements of fasting I drew our attention to in our definition of *fasting* in the previous chapters are each present in the Day of Atonement requirements. First, this is a grievous sacred moment of confessing sin and finding atonement and forgiveness. Second, Israel's response to the sacredness of this moment is to deny itself of food as well as physical comfort and pleasure. Third, the whole person engages in the act of repentance—not just the heart or the soul or the mind or the spirit. Yom Kippur was a day when Israel responded to God's holy repudiation of sin, took on God's very own *pathos*, and acted out their repentance in fasting.

What about us? Does Yom Kippur have anything to do with Christian living today? I see no reason why we can't set aside a day to respond to our own sin and to our need for repentance annually. Some might want to attach such an event to the Jewish calendar to express a Christian variant of Yom Kippur. But something else is more natural for us. We could enliven Lent or at least Good Friday by bringing body and soul into harmony together as we turn from sin and learn to face God with a more holistic integrity through an absolute fast and even some practices of self-denial. If our shame over our sin arises in the heart of our very being or finds itself lodged in the core of our conscience—and most of us know just how penetrating this experience is—and if the body and heart are one, depriving ourselves of food and denying ourselves simple pleasures manifest themselves naturally.

Regret awakens in me when I think of what a more unified perception of the body and spirit would do for the church today. During Lent, many of us give up something—a modern equivalent of "afflicting oneself." Some abstain from all beverages besides water, while others (perhaps the majority) abstain from chocolate or desserts or candies or sugary drinks. These minor self-afflictions or abstinences, if done properly, can become iconic in that they can open us up to the larger themes of sin, the need for repentance, and the coming glorious celebration of forgiveness we discover during Holy Week.

WHEN GOD SEEMS ABSENT

Most of us know the dryness of prayer or the low ceiling off which some of our prayers seem to bounce. Some mornings we wake up to discover that we seem to have lost God's very presence in our lives. What to do? The wisdom of the ages is that sensitive people fast to communicate with God during dry days. A biblical story about Ichabod and Ebenezer shows how dry days of God's absence led Israel to a sacred moment of repentance. And because they rightly responded to the sacred moment, they found the glorious result of God's blessed presence again. What we get in this story is an image, the image of the ark of the covenant. That ark represents God's presence, and this story can become our story.

Early in Israel's history, during the time of Samuel, the ark of God was captured by Israel's pesky enemies, the Philistines. When the news of the ark's captivity reached Eli, the ninety-eight-year-old judge who had guided Israel for forty years, he fell over backward, broke his neck, and died. For Eli, that ark represented the presence and blessing of God. For him, God had left God's people. Eli's daughter-in-law responded to Eli's death by going into labor and giving birth to a son whom she named Ichabod—"The glory [of God] has departed (1 Sam. 4)."

Yet one person's response is not the whole story. The absence of the ark embodied the absence of God's blessing on Israel. A few chapters later, Samuel recognized the solemnity of this moment of the ark's absence and what it meant for God's blessing. So Samuel arose to challenge Israel to worship the one and only God, YHWH. Samuel summoned all Israel to Mizpah, where he prayed for them and called them to respond to God's absence by fasting. "So they gathered at Mizpah, and drew water and poured it out before the LORD. They *fasted* that day, and said, 'We have sinned against the LORD.' And Samuel judged the people of Israel at Mizpah" (1 Sam. 7:6; emphasis added). That day Israel found victory over the Philistines and over the false gods, and so Samuel set up a stone and called it Ebenezer—"Stone of [God's] help " (v. 12).

It would be easy here to focus on the B (fasting) ➔ C (return of God) columns and to come away with the idea that if we fast, we might experience a greater presence of God. And that might be true. But let's remind ourselves again of our definition of fasting: *fasting is the natural, inevitable response of a person to a grievous sacred moment in life.* What we should see in the Ichabod and Ebenezer story is not so much that fasting can trigger the return of God's blessing, but how Samuel and Israel *responded* to the absence of the ark and the absence of God's blessing. We dare not forget the A column, the sacred moment involved in the act of fasting. Because the Israelites yearned for God's presence, they fasted; that yearning was blessed by God.

I believe we can learn from this by focusing not so much on what we want but on the grievous nature of the moment. If we sense the absence of God, I believe we are in a sacred moment.

We need to let this very absence of God create in us a sense of yearning for God's presence, and fasting is one thing we can do to respond to and embody that absence of God. Instead of seeing fasting as an instrument that can bring God back, we need to see fasting as what unified persons naturally do when they encounter an experience of God's absence. So instead of looking to C, we need to look to A.

WHEN WE REALIZE COMPLICITY

I'll never forget a student who, after listening to a lecture I gave on Jesus and the poor, came to me with her eyes suddenly wide open: "Never in my life, even though I grew up in a church, did I realize how materialistic I have become and how it hurts others. I feel sick about my life." How many of us have watched a TV show, read a news report, or scanned the Internet and found ourselves face-to-face with our own billowy comfort in the teeth of abject misery on the part of others?

A little more than a year after Hurricane Katrina buckled the knees of the Gulf Coast, I was in New Orleans and saw houses that had a spray-painted grid with numbers of bodies found. Most of the former residents of New Orleans have not returned to their houses, thousands of houses are still standing empty and may never be filled, and many of the schools have not reopened. As Dr. Bill Warren, a professor at New Orleans Baptist

Theological Seminary, drove me around some neighborhoods, I was stunned. I felt complicit in this impoverishment because I didn't know how bad it still was. But I was heartened by the efforts of Bill and his colleagues and students and community.

What should we do? How should we respond when we are confronted by such poverty? The Bible's wisdom reveals that people in tune with God fast in such a situation. They fast in order to become more compassionate. In a later chapter we will look at *body poverty*, but for now we merely observe that a genuine response to our own moral insensitivities and our complicity in systemic evil is fasting. I confess to you that fasting didn't even enter my mind as I wandered through New Orleans.

Think of Israel's return from exile and the rebuilding of the temple and its walls under the leadership of Ezra and Nehemiah. When Ezra realized how many Israelites had intermarried with foreign women in overt disobedience to what the Torah taught, he was overcome with grief. Realizing his complicity, Ezra withdrew from the house of God to spend the night alone before God. No moment was more solemn in all of Ezra's life, so he "did not eat bread or drink water, for he was mourning over the faithlessness of the exiles" (Ezra 10:6). Fasting was Ezra's way of demonstrating his own complicity in Israel's moral wandering, and it was also his way of identifying with his fellow wanderers from God in order to lift them before the God of mercy. In other words, fasting was Ezra's way of identifying with God's will for God's people. Ezra here was caught up in the

A → B columns, the sacred moment of recognizing complicity in sin and the response of fasting. His fasting was not done to get something but to respond to a grievous situation.

Many of us are moved emotionally by the realization of needs and our complicity in poverty, but we are far too often more moved emotionally than we are moved to do something about it. Fasting might be the best way for many of us to seal the moment; fasting for a day might be what we most need to change our own pathetic passivity in the face of famine. It might be the way for each of us to bring our entire person in line with God's heart for the poor.

AT CONVERSION AND BAPTISM

Statistics show that most Christian conversions in the Western world occur through families—families who baptized their children as infants and nurtured them into the faith or who led their family members into a personal decision to follow Christ. In fact, a recent study by Andrew Greeley and Michael Hout, called *The Truth About Conservative Christians*, contends that the major reason conservative churches are growing is because conservative moms are more fertile.[1] So when my Democrat friends complain about the rise of conservatives, I sometimes suggest they teach their kids to have more babies! Because most conversions occur through the gradual socializing process of being nurtured into the faith,

33

the starker realities of repentance can easily fall into the footnotes of history. This has led in many churches to an almost total disconnect between conversion and fasting. I'm all for nurturing our children into the faith—my wife, Kris, and I did our best with our children, Laura and Lukas. But a concern with nurturing faith ought not to lead us too far from the value of connecting fasting to conversion. Baptism is a great time for body turning.

Most of us know the story of Saul-become-Paul's conversion—he saw the Lord, and his eyes must have twittered and his body must have shaken. But there is more to the story than Saul's encountering the risen Lord, entering into Damascus, and not being able to see anything for three days. Alongside these well-known details, the author of Acts tells us that Saul "neither ate nor drank" for three days (Acts 9:9). So sacred was his moment of seeing Jesus, so powerful was his realization that he had been opposing the very work of God, so potent was his apprehension of his sin, and so deeply did he sense God's grief over his sinfulness, that Saul repented with an absolute fast for three days.

Conversion and fasting seem to have been a natural couple from the very start of the church. Here is a text from an early Christian document called Didache, written in either the late first century or early second century: "And before the baptism, let the one baptizing and the one who is to be baptized fast, as well as any others who are able. Also, you must instruct the one who is to be baptized to fast for one or two days beforehand" (Did. 7:4). Notice that not only did the convert fast, but also the one who baptized, as did "any others who are able." In our own modern world, the Roman Catholic Rite of Christian Initiation for Adults (RCIA) reflects the world of Paul and the earliest Christians. Entrance into the Church involves instruction (cate-chesis), introspection (fasting during Lent), and then participa-tion in the Easter vigil service (receiving the sacrament). The need to order the conversion experience during Lent and Easter is too structured, in my opinion. Still, the elements of conver-sion (instruction, introspection leading to repentance, and par-ticipation) emphasized in the Catholic rite of initiation remain central for conversion—and one observes that fasting finds its way into the heart of the mix. Conversion is above all a serious sacred moment to which one naturally responds with fasting.

I recommend that we reconsider the absence of fasting in the conversion process today. Of course, local churches will have to work this out for themselves, but the wisdom of the Bible and the church clearly urges us to rethink our practices.

AN APPEAL FOR BODY TURNING

Whenever the people of God need to be reminded of their solemn duty to turn away from sin and to face the Lord of light—during Lent or following the realization of some sin, whether public or private, whether corporate or personal—the words of Joel the prophet remind us what to do:

Yet even now, says the LORD,

 return to me with all your heart,

with fasting, with weeping, and with mourning;

 rend your hearts and not your clothing.

Return to the LORD, your God,

 for he is gracious and merciful,

slow to anger, and abounding in steadfast love,

 and relents from punishing.

Who knows whether he will not turn and relent,

 and leave a blessing behind him,

a grain offering and a drink offering

 for the LORD, your God?

Blow the trumpet in Zion;

 sanctify a *fast*;

  call a solemn assembly. (Joel 2:12–15; emphasis added)

Fasting is body turning from sin to faithful devotion to God; it is body talk of the entire person at home with itself in a body. Above all, body turning is the natural response of the biblical faith to the sacred moment of sin, repentance, conversion, and the healing graces of forgiveness. In the next chapter, we will explore how prayer itself, pleading with God, naturally finds its way into fasting.

4

FASTING AS
BODY PLEA

MANY YOUNG CHRISTIANS TODAY WORSHIP IN WAYS I
never did. They raise their hands, they dance, they sway, and
they act out the words of their worship. I am aware of my discomfort with their practices because I was nurtured in a dis-
embodied form of worship and the Christian faith. But this
new generation seems to be catching on to the biblical perception of the whole person wholly engaged with God. I believe
there is a growing surge of whole-body spirituality at work in
the Christian West today, and current worship practices are
part of that resurgence. For my generation, the whole person
was what went on *inside* the body, in the secret recesses of the
soul and spirit and mind. What is going on in many churches
today is much more embodied than my generation's worship
style, and this emerging generation encourages me to think that

bodies are being fused with spiritual acts. A widespread appreciation of fasting may follow—and if some reports are accurate, it has already arrived for some.

In the Bible, pleas and supplications and prayers were accompanied by the embodied act of fasting. Why? Once again because of a response to a grievous sacred moment. The biblical and Christian tradition encourages us to plead with fasting in response to five sacred moments. So, once again, we will keep our focus in this chapter on some biblical teachings about what I'm calling *body plea*. We begin with how national moral disasters led ancient Israelites to body plea.

NATIONAL MORAL DISASTERS

What was the proper initial response to the holocaust in Germany during World War II? to the holocaust in Rwanda? to the evils in Darfur? to the violence in Kenya? Or to international conflicts such as those in Afghanistan and Iraq? Or even to our vicarious participation in moral corruption, as when we read something like Azar Nafisi's *Reading Lolita in Tehran* or Alan Paton's classic *Cry, the Beloved Country*?[1] What do you do when the world around is collapsing around you or when evil and injustice seem to overwhelm the good and the just? One biblical story points the way even for us today.

A LEVITE, A CONCUBINE,
AND THE MEN OF GIBEAH

We might consider the story about the Levite (an attendant at Israel's sacred worship center) and his concubine wife, found in Judges 19–20, a story when immorality buckled the knees of the people of God. The concubine wife was from Bethlehem of Judah; the Levite husband was from Ephraim. The concubine, true to her former calling, was unfaithful to the Levite and returned to Bethlehem. The Levite sought her out, found her, and headed back with her to Ephraim. On the first night, they made it as far as Gibeah in Benjamin, where an elderly man offered them hospitality. When the males of Gibeah heard that a Levite was spending the night in their midst, they demanded to have sexual intercourse with him. The man—the Levite—gave the rabble his concubine-wife, whom they raped and abused throughout the night. The woman found the strength to return to the old man's house but collapsed at the doorway. The Levite, untrue to his own calling, said, "Get up; let's go." She didn't answer; the abused woman was dead. So he lifted her onto his donkey. When he got home, he cut her into twelve pieces and sent a chunk of her body to each of the twelve tribes of Israel.

The response to this hideous story? "Such a thing has never been seen or done . . . Tell us what to do!" (see Judg. 19:30).

The moral fabric of a nation had been shredded with moral violence. What were they to do?

WHAT TO DO?

"Then all the Israelites . . . went back to Bethel and wept, sitting there before the LORD; *they fasted that day until evening.* They then offered burnt offerings and sacrifices of well-being before the LORD . . . and inquired of the LORD" (Judg. 20:26–27; emphasis added). In the midst of this depravity and perversity—rape and murder and war and delight in death—we find the secret of fasting: a moment so grievously and shockingly sacred that the Israelites could not even eat. All they could think about was repenting from their sins and pleading with God for justice.

The story sickens me. Even if the "good guy" wins and some semblance of order is reestablished in this biblical story, I come away from the text the way I do when I read *The Iliad* or Samuel Butler's *The Way of All Flesh* or when Kris and I watched the intense movie *Fatal Attraction.* Victory, yes, but at what cost? Isn't it perverse to enter into stories filled with blood and death and violence? So, too, with this biblical narrative. The only response to the grievous situation is repentance and fasting and confession and pleading with God to show mercy. That response of confession, of body turning accompanied by body plea, can lead to grace, forgiveness, and a reordering of moral fabric.

God's people, when they encounter a grievous sacred moment in which the moral fabric of society begins to unravel, engage themselves in body plea. Body, spirit, and soul weld themselves into a unified action, the whole person facing God and pleading for grace and mercy and justice.

THE FAILURE OF OTHERS

I love Moses. He seems such a real and robust and round character—he did both stupid things and brilliant things but kept going on with God all the way to the end. If you say one thing about Moses, it has to be that he was focused on God. God honored him by giving Moses the first edition of the Ten Commandments. Moses also had the heart of a pastor-priest: he cared so much about God that he went to bat for his people before God. He knew so much about Israel that Moses feared what God might do to them for their idolatries. Moses knew the moral core of Israel was disintegrating and disappearing. In that grievous sacred moment, Moses responded with fasting.

So serious was Moses about his obligation to intercede that he tells us all about his body plea before God:

> So I took hold of the two tablets and flung them from my two
> hands, smashing them before your eyes. Then I lay prostrate
> before the LORD as before, *forty days and forty nights; I neither ate*

bread nor drank water, because of all the sin you had committed, provoking the LORD by doing what was evil in his sight.
For I was afraid that the anger that the LORD bore against
you was so fierce that he would destroy you. But the LORD lis-
tened to me that time also. The LORD was so angry with
Aaron that he was ready to destroy him, but I interceded also
on behalf of Aaron at that same time. Then I took the sinful
thing you had made, the calf, and burned it with fire and
crushed it, grinding it thoroughly, until it was reduced to dust;
and I threw the dust of it into the stream that runs down the
mountain. (Deut. 9:17–21; emphasis added)

Moses was fired up with God's absolute holiness, and he
knew that the biggest sin of all was to worship false gods, so he
interceded for his "congregation" by fasting for forty days and
nights. This scene in the Bible is graphically concrete and physical and embodied—God and Moses, the golden calf, fasting,
and grinding up the golden calf and tossing the dust into the
stream.

How do we respond when we discover the fresh, fatal sins
of others? This story about Moses' body pleading speaks
against our tendency to publicize our complaints about others.
We have become a culture of cultural critics and a church of
church critics. Perhaps more of us need to be quick to convert
our concern about the moral failures of others into body pleading for them instead of public words against them. Perhaps our

concern for our nation's failures would be best expressed by joining Jehoshaphat, Nehemiah, Esther, and Anna in fasting for our country and counties and their leaders and citizens.[2]

THE HEALTH OF OTHERS

The Christian tradition encourages us to turn to body plea not only for national and moral collapses, but also for the health of others. Why? Because sickness evokes death, one of life's most grievous sacred moments. Body pleading for the health of others emphasizes again the essence of fasting: it is not about manipulating a situation by fasting but about *responding* to a grievous sacred moment.

Pete Greig is a founding leader of 24-7prayer.com, a ministry that escalated from a one-time prayer room event into an international commitment by Christians to plead with God in prayer. Pete was also considered to be one of the top fifty revolutionary leaders by *Relevant* magazine.[3] One night Samie, Pete's wife, woke him up with convulsions. Pete heard this question from the one he loved: "What's happening to me?" Her eyes, he tells us, had turned from summer-blue to "moons of white" and she pleaded with her husband: "P-p-p-pray." Pete says, "And so I did. I prayed like I'd never prayed before, helplessly convinced that I was watching my wife die. I begged God to make the convulsions stop so that she could at least draw breath." Pete prayed every way he'd ever prayed but, as he confesses, "My prayers weren't working."

Samie had a brain tumor; her tumor was operable. She recovered (mostly), and their life has gone on, but it is not the same. Pete's prayers to preserve the life of his dear wife were answered. Pete's book, *God on Mute: Engaging the Silence of Unanswered Prayer*, which is the book Samie admits she wanted as she has undergone surgeries and struggles to maintain an ordinary life, sketches why God doesn't always answer our prayers the way we'd like.[4]

But unanswered prayers do not stop us from praying for those whom we love. The saints of the Bible famously faced God in prayer to plead for the health of others—and very frequently they fasted to express their body plea. Take David, for example. David was "the man" at whom Nathan, the prophet, pointed when exposing the nasty incident when David took Uriah's wife and then had Uriah murdered (2 Sam. 12:7). And the judgment Nathan announced was that David's dear son would die. David's *response* to the sudden illness of his son, and his complicity in that death, was this: he pleaded with God by fasting, prostrating himself on the floor all night long, and refusing fellowship with friends—and he did this for an entire week. God did not "hear" his prayer, and God did not change his mind, but that did not stop David in his body plea (2 Sam. 12:15–19).

To this day, even when we know the odds are against us, we do not cease from our own intercessions for the health of others.

Fasting makes these prayers doubly real. As I write this sentence, someone I admire—Dr. Robert Webber—sits in his home in Michigan with Joanne, his wife, as he suffers from cancer. The doctor gave him a few weeks well before Christmas in 2006; we are now beginning to sense the warming breezes of spring in Chicago in 2007, and Bob is still with us. The odds are against him, but family and friends are praying and pleading with God, some with fasting (as I have done), that God will preserve his life. (Indeed, on April 27, 2007, the Lord chose to take Bob home. But this does not discourage the church from body pleading.)

Fasting as body pleading for those we love is natural. But David even prayed for the health of his *enemies*, a revolutionary body plea that could make a dramatic impact in our world. The early Christian document called Didache follows David in this body plea and urges Christians to "fast for those who persecute you" (Did. 1:4). Back to David's words:

Malicious witnesses rise up;
    they ask me about things I do not know.
They repay me evil for good;
    my soul is forlorn.
But as for me, when they were sick,
    I wore sackcloth;
    I afflicted myself with fasting.
I prayed with head bowed on my bosom,
    as though I grieved for a friend or a brother;

> *I went about as one who laments for a mother,*
>
>> *bowed down and in mourning.* (Ps. 35:11–14, emphasis added)

Enemies can become friends if they hear we are fasting for their healing. Body plea might be one of world peace's most unlocked secrets.

There are at least two more reasons we might think more of attaching fasting to our pleading with God.

THE DESIRES OF OUR HEARTS

Sometimes we want something; sometimes we need something. And sometimes we want something so much we convert our wants into body plea. Wants and needs get wrapped into an "I must have this, and I will not let go" situation.

In 1 Samuel 1:1–20, we see an example of one woman's desperate desire that became a body plea before God. Hannah wanted a baby; she felt she had waited long enough. To make matters worse, when she and her husband, Elkanah, went annually to the worship center, Elkanah (out of mercy) gave Hannah a double portion for sacrifice—one for her and one for the baby she did not have. This only intensified Hannah's pain. On top of this pain, Elkanah also had another wife—as so many had in those days—and his other wife, Peninnah, had children of her own and sometimes chided Hannah for her barrenness.

Hannah's barren condition was seen by some to be a judgment from God, but she knew in her own heart it wasn't. So Hannah prayed and fasted. She went to the altar at Shiloh with her body plea and wept in prayer. She did what millions before and after have done: she bargained with God. "If only you will look on the misery of your servant, and remember me, and . . . give to your servant a male child, then I will set him before you as a nazirite until the day of his death" (v. 11).

Hannah's example has been followed by millions. In a day when fasting has fallen so far from favor, Hannah might become an example of a sacred desire being expressed by a unified person by pleading with God through fasting. Notice again that her fasting was a *response* to a grievous condition— barrenness. She responded to her barrenness with fasting in the hope that God would answer her, which God did.

THE GUIDANCE FROM OUR GOD

Students routinely make appointments with me to discuss "God's will" for their lives. Once a student was having a particularly hard time figuring out what to do next, so I advised a day or two of fasting—to which he suggested, upon further reflection, that he thought he had God's will already figured out!

On a more serious note, when we are facing a fork in the road or even a slippery path through unknown terrain on a dark night, the wisdom of fasting proves itself as a secure method for gaining clarity and the Lord's blessing, because fasting expresses the unified person facing God in prayer. That statement brings together all three columns—the A column of a sacred moment, the B column of fasting, and the C column of God's response. The A column's serious sacred moment is mystery, the unknown, the desire to know with clarity what God has called us to do.

When the children of Israel (Judah) had been in Babylon too long and were on the verge of returning under the leadership of Ezra, they fasted. Right there at the river Ahava near Babylon, they denied themselves the comforts and pleasures they were used to and fasted in order to plead with God for guidance and protection as they made the long trek back to the promised land (Ezra 8:21–23). Ezra, man of faith that he was, was ashamed to ask the king for soldiers to protect God's people, so he sought the Lord in prayer for that protection. He got it, and God's people finally returned home.

Centuries later, Saul (later known as Paul) was part of the burgeoning Christian movement. The gathering of Christians in Antioch included some prophets and teachers, and they were worshiping *and fasting* when God, through the Holy Spirit, uttered a word that began what can only be called the most significant missionary tour in the history of the church: "'Set apart for me Barnabas and Saul for the work to which I have called them.' Then after fasting and praying, they laid their hands on them and sent them off" (Acts 13:2–3). This fasting gave rise to specific guidance from God, but it was a response to the serious condition of not knowing what to do.

The emphasis of these passages in the Bible is not that fasting clears the mind and opens the windows for God's light to enter. Instead, the emphasis is on *the yearning of God's people to know God's will.* They are focused on the sacred moment more than on the use of fasting as an instrument to get what they want. To be sure, they wanted something and they pleaded with God to get it, but I want to emphasize that there is a genuine spiritual balance here: these good folks encountered the serious sacredness of wanting to know God's will, and that yearning prompted their body plea.

AN ENCOURAGEMENT

Fasting along with our prayer requests is not some kind of magic bullet to ensure the answer we want. Fasting doesn't reinforce the crumbling walls of our prayers like a flying buttress, nor is it a manipulative device. We fast because a condition arises—what we are calling the sacred moment—that leads us to desire something deeply. We fast because our plea is so intense that in the midst of our sacred desire eating seems sacrilegious.

A body plea occurs when the unified person gives himself or herself wholly to God to plead for something or someone. There is an ancient biblical tradition that flows well beyond the river

Ahava into the entire history of the church to urge faithful Christians to engage in body plea. Sometimes, to quote James, the brother of Jesus, we have not because we ask not. And sometimes we have not because we don't want it bad enough (James 4:2). Fasting can be the way for the unified person to turn to God to plead with God completely.

5

FASTING AS
BODY GRIEF

I HAVE OBSERVED THAT WHEN SOMEONE DIES, A DEEP instinct triggers an impulse for everyone to do two things: to stifle the desire to eat and, at the same time, to bring food to the family. And every funeral I've been to finishes when the family and friends join together for a meal at the local church. Eating together as an expression of our love for one another, and especially in our support of the grieving family, seems reasonable. Eating together after a funeral breaks the initial stunning shock of death, which often prompts fasting, and it joins us together to face the future.

Furthermore, the custom of friends bringing food to a family during bereavement expresses the very heart of what fasting as body talk is all about. The natural and inevitable response to the death of a loved one, surely one of life's most grievous sacred moments, is to shut down the desires that bring pleasure, like eating. To continue our A ➜ B ➜ C framework, body grief is entirely a response (B) to a grievous situation (A), and not at all an instrument to bring some kind of reward (C). I believe body grief is at the foundation of all fasting practices, and if we learn to think of fasting as a response to a grievous sacred moment, it all falls into place. And, as we will see in the chapters that follow, the responsive nature of fasting actually clarifies some of the problems and misunderstandings that have become attached to the history of fasting among Christians.

Why fast when someone dies? Because our respect for the person who has died is so immense and our grief so great that indulgence in any kind of pleasure desacralizes that respect and pain. Instead of drowning our sorrow in drink or flushing it away with foods, the sober person drinks the pain of death and offers the gift of grace to the bereaved with utter clarity by remaining fully alert through fasting. Furthermore, body grief is also an act of empathy with the grieving family. The discomfort that comes from fasting evokes in the bereaved a compassionate identification with the family and comforts the family as support. Let me say this again: the pain of someone's death is so intense, or the moment so bleak, or the sense of the unknown so profound, or the encounter with God so deep, that we find eating a distraction from memories of the one who has died, the experience of the grieving family, and the reality of mortality. Sadness so consumes us that we forget about eating.

The sacredness of the moment is palpable; eating seems

sacrilegious. This theme is found throughout the Bible and the Christian tradition.

DAVID AND HIS GRIEF-STRICKEN WORLD

David wrote music and sang songs as Israel's king. But because he lived in turbulent times, he witnessed a great deal of death and so was filled with grief, along with those around him. David's best friend was Jonathan, and Jonathan's father was Saul, the first king of Israel.

David was destined to fill Saul's role as king, but Saul hated the prospect of losing his power. So he plotted to kill David. One day Saul expressed outrage at his son Jonathan because of the young man's loyalty to David. So outraged was he that he tried to kill Jonathan with his spear. If Saul was willing to kill his own son for liking David, then the prospects of David's survival were dismal indeed.

This brush with his father's plans led Jonathan to the response of fasting over the inevitable death of his best friend, David (1 Sam. 20:34). Notice how the Bible says this: "Jonathan rose from the table in fierce anger and ate no food on the second day of the month, for he was grieved for David, and because his father had disgraced him." Jonathan's fast was not connected to body pleading to preserve either his or David's life. Instead, Jonathan's fast is what we found throughout the

Bible: a *response* to a grievous situation. He was so shaken by what he thought was the certain, imminent death of his friend David and the shame his father was bringing down on him that he began to fast for David.

Not long after this episode, the Bible tells us about the death of Saul himself (1 Sam. 31). The Philistines killed Jonathan and his brothers in battle. Then Saul, who had been injured, begged his own armor-bearer to thrust a sword into him so that he might die before his enemies could disgrace him by putting him to death in some humiliating manner. The armor-bearer refused, so Saul committed suicide. Saul's death was not enough for the zealous and vengeful Philistines when they found Saul's body and hung on the wall of Beth-shan. When news of this disgrace found its way to the Israelites, some valiant men of Jabesh-Gilead recaptured the disgraced body of Saul and those of his sons, brought them home, and then fasted for seven days (v. 13). Again, body grieving here is a response to death and not a discipline performed to gain something. This responsive element is at the heart of the great spiritual traditions about fasting.

David had already developed a lifestyle of fasting for his enemies, so he grieved over the death of Saul and his sons, but especially over Jonathan. To express that grief, David fasted for Saul and his family and for the whole nation (2 Sam 1:12). David's own military leader, Joab, murdered Saul's military leader, Abner. When this happened, David fasted once again in grief over a death (3:35). This time he and his people rent their clothing and put on sackcloth to afflict themselves in their grief.

Alongside such examples of fasting, the ancients grieved in ways that seem extravagant to us today. Death could bring on, besides the above-mentioned rending of clothes and wearing of sackcloth, messing up one's hair or even pulling gobs of it out, tossing dust on one's head and clothing, or even wallowing around in the dust. Even if those methods are not ours, grief is one of our fundamental realities. Sometimes we are surprised with how realistic the Bible can be, and the following psalm reminds us of how real grieving was (and is).

THE GRIEVING PROCESS IN PSALM 77

One day in reading aloud from the Psalms, I was struck by Psalm 77. What I found in this psalm was a person who moved from the depths of grief to a settled confidence that God was not absent. The psalmist discovered that the seeming absence of God could be countered by recognizing the actual presence of God in what he had experienced as God's absence. In light of what we have said so far in this book, I would like to claim Psalm 77 as the Faster's Prayer. The fundamental responsive nature of fasting, even though fasting is not directly mentioned, finds its natural words in this psalm. These are the kinds of words that came out of the ancient Israelites and Christians when fasting was the normal response.

The first three verses of this psalm, written by Asaph, express the reality of Asaph's grief; he is incapable of doing anything but moaning over a grievous situation.

> I cry aloud to God,
>> aloud to God, that he may hear me.
> In the day of my trouble I seek the Lord;
>> in the night my hand is stretched out without wearying;
>> my soul refuses to be comforted.
> I think of God, and I moan;
>> I meditate, and my spirit faints. (vv. 1–3)

Those who grieve are not afraid to say what's on the heart and in the depth of the soul. In the last two lines above, Asaph says that even thinking of God makes him moan! That's honesty before God.

Asaph now turns his complaint to God: he blames God for his condition, and he thinks of how often he ponders how God used to act. Then he wonders if God even cares, and laments that God has changed from being a merciful God to a distant, uncaring God (vv. 4–10). Asaph has some big questions for God that emerge from his grievous situation.

> You keep my eyelids from closing;
>> I am so troubled that I cannot speak.

I consider the days of old,

and remember the years of long ago.

I commune with my heart in the night;

I meditate and search my spirit:

"Will the Lord spurn forever,

and never again be favorable?

Has his steadfast love ceased forever?

Are his promises at an end for all time?

Has God forgotten to be gracious?

Has he in anger shut up his compassion?" (vv. 4–9)

Though Asaph does not mention fasting in this psalm, what he describes here is the kind of grievous sacred moment that prompts fasting. Grieving in response to such a sacred moment gives way now to a reflection on how God has acted in the past. We sense Asaph's faith (and relief?) in verses 10–20 as he thinks his way into and through his own grief.

And I say, "It is my grief

that the right hand of the Most High has changed."

I will call to mind the deeds of the LORD;

I will remember your wonders of old.

I will meditate on all your work,

and muse on your mighty deeds.

Your way, O God, is holy.

What god is so great as our God?

You are the God who works wonders;

    you have displayed your might among the peoples.

With your strong arm you redeemed your people,

    the descendants of Jacob and Joseph. *Selah*

When the waters saw you, O God,

    when the waters saw you, they were afraid;

    the very deep trembled.

The clouds poured out water;

    the skies thundered;

    your arrows flashed on every side.

The crash of your thunder was in the whirlwind;

    your lightnings lit up the world;

    the earth trembled and shook.

Your way was through the sea,

    your path, through the mighty waters;

    yet your footprints were unseen.

You led your people like a flock

    by the hand of Moses and Aaron.

The genius of the Israelite and Christian understanding of fasting is all here: Asaph did not grieve (and probably fast) in order to find relief. He grieved because he sensed the severity of a sacred moment—and he doesn't tell us the details. His grief was definitely an A ➜ B movement. Asaph was overwhelmed by what was going on and what was not going on around him. He was convinced that God ought to be doing something, but God wasn't.

In this psalm, we can observe a glimmer of hope in Asaph: he seemed to have found a way through his grievous situation into relief by pondering the ways of God in Israel's history.

GRIEF AND FASTING

Books on fasting rarely do more than mention fasting and grief, even though grief may be the thread that connects all kinds of fasting. One might say that body turning expresses a grief over one's sins so profound that the person refuses to eat; further, many of our body pleas with God originate in grief over a condition that we find intolerable or a request that drives us to an inability to be satisfied until we have spent time in God's presence. And even disciplinary fasting (body discipline), which concerns an ongoing life of seeking to grow in love and holiness and which is the subject of our next chapter, often grows in the tear-moistened soil of grief over own lack of love or our selfishness or the same failures in the world around us.

Recent scholars have emphasized eschatology as a driving force in fasting as body hope. Namely, Jesus (as we will discuss in chapter 10) said that the Jewish practice of fasting as an anticipation of the kingdom was to be temporarily suspended as long as he—the bridegroom and his presence of the king-dom—was with them. But after he had returned to the Father, that fasting would resume (Luke 5:35). It is not uncommon for a fast motivated by a yearning for kingdom justice to be simul-taneously motivated by grief over the absence of justice, peace, and love in this world in the here and now.

Grief, then, is not the exotic aunt of fasting who, because she is unfortunately and uncomfortably part of the family, has to be invited to the home for the holiday. Not at all. Body grief is perhaps the purest example of what fasting is all about: a human being, overwhelmed by the sacredness of a moment, chooses not to eat in order to sanctify his or her communion with God and participate fully in one of life's grievous moments.

The most misunderstood aspect of fasting is found in our next chapter, what I call *body discipline*—the choice to deny one's body food in order to conquer sinful desires and become more holy. If body discipline learns to focus on the grievous sacred moment that prompts the discipline, we will discover the secret to the most common form of fasting in the world's religions, not the least of which is the Christian tradition of disciplinary fasting.

6

FASTING AS
BODY DISCIPLINE

ONE OF THE MOST CHARMING AND BEST BOOKS WRITTEN
on fasting is by Adalbert de Vogüé, a monk of the Abbey of La
Pierre-qui-Vire in France. His small book, *To Love Fasting: The
Monastic Experience,* is a near-perfect expression of body discipline.[1] In fact, so gentle is his disciplinary fasting practice that I
hesitate to call his form of fasting "body discipline." *To Love
Fasting* is just that—to delight in a life regulated by sacred
rhythms and fasting. The best way to describe body discipline
is to tell the story of this monk.

The monk arises at three a.m., celebrates the night office of
prayer and reading for an hour and a half, and then spends the
morning in duties that include four hours or so of study. He
does not eat breakfast or lunch, but at noontime he spends time
with his community of faith and then returns to his hermitage
with a box of food for dinner. He spends his afternoon in study
and celebrating the afternoon office of prayer. He spends an

hour in manual work and then walks and meditates. As the twenty-four hours since his last meal nears, he observes this: "My mind is at its most lucid, my body vigorous and well disposed, my heart light and full of joy."[2] He eats an evening dinner at 6:30 p.m. and it takes him nearly an hour, reading as he eats. He then celebrates Vespers, cleans up, does the Compline office, and goes to sleep. For some, de Vogüé's life is idyllic.

Adalbert de Vogüé fasts in order to foster spiritual formation. In light of our previous chapters, it should be observed that his fasting is not about repentance or grief or supplication, and we'll say more about this later. But de Vogüé's fasting is not so much an A → B form of fasting, as a B → C form. His fasting life is the joyful rhythm of near solitude. It gives him "happy afternoons" and a "deep influence on my whole moral life." Sexual fantasies seem to disappear, as do other irritating emotions. Furthermore, there is clearly an *instrumental* element to his fasting. As he describes it, "I think the cause [of my joy] is that a certain mastery of the primordial appetite, eating, permits a greater mastery of the other manifestations of the libido and aggressiveness. It is as if the man who fasts were more himself, in possession of his true identity, and less dependent on exterior objects and the impulses they arouse in him."[3] He is aware of his unique vocation and situation as a monk whose life is not challenged by a multitude of family and busyness and distractions. Still, with his pastoral eye on the nonmonastic Christian, he makes this suggestion: "I think it healthy to keep in training by the search for the truly necessary minimum [of food]."[4] Recently an Anglican rector friend of mine, Rob Merola, said this to me when we were discussing some of the themes of this book: "You'd be surprised how little food we actually need."

Even if you idealize the life of de Vogüé, even if you know the benefits of this kind of life for yourself, and even if you would like this kind of life but can't make it happen, the disciplinary fasting he advocates cannot be found explicitly in the pages of the Bible. Yet body discipline as an *instrumental* form of fasting is perhaps the most common understanding of fasting. It also sometimes leads to the most common misunderstanding of fasting, that we fast in order to get something. So we need to examine the biblical and early Christian foundations for the development of body discipline.

Just in case you are wondering, I don't believe body discipline is wrong. But I do think it can be enriched by our understanding of the A ➔ B ➔ C approach. More attention needs to be given by proponents of body discipline to the A column—to the grievous sacred moments that prompt fasting as a daily, rather than occasional, response.

A PLACE TO BEGIN

Perhaps if we read the following prayer from the Anglican Book of Common Prayer, we can find the most important sacred moment grievous enough to establish body discipline. In fact, I believe body discipline finds its genius in the ideas and theology inherent in this ageless prayer:

Almighty God,

You know that we have no power in ourselves to help ourselves: Keep me both outwardly in my body and inwardly in my soul, that I may be defended from all adversities which may happen to the body, and from all evil thoughts which may assault and hurt the soul.

Through Jesus Christ our Lord, who lives and reigns with you and the Holy Spirit, one God, for ever and ever.

Amen.

The foundational sacred moment for body discipline is consciousness of sin, consciousness of weakness, the need for God's empowering grace, the desire to cut back in life in order to find our center, and a yearning to grow morally in love and holiness. In this prayer we see some dualistic thinking—"outwardly in my body and inwardly in my soul"—but it does not necessarily fall into the trap of dualism, of thinking the latter is important and the former unimportant. When the integral connection of body and soul is affirmed, body discipline begins to wave its hand as a viable and spiritually forming discipline. When we spend more time pondering our moral weaknesses and our desire to be transformed, suddenly body discipline becomes natural and desired.

So from this prayer we can learn this: if we take our mortal condition and our moral life seriously, if we realize that our body and our soul (or spirit) are integrally connected, then the very physical act of body discipline is as natural as fasting in response to death or repentance. In fact, body discipline is designed—if we think about it seriously—as a life of ongoing repentance in the face of ongoing moral development.

Body discipline did not come to full fruition until the second, third, and fourth centuries after Christ, but the question is whether it was already found among the earliest Christians. Let's take a look.

PAUL AND BODY DISCIPLINE

Notice the apostle Paul's revealing confession in the ninth chapter of his first letter to the churches at Corinth. In this passage, we might see an example of body discipline:

> Do you not know that in a race the runners all compete, but only one receives the prize? Run in such a way that you may win it. Athletes exercise self-control in all things; they do it to receive a perishable wreath, but we an imperishable one. So I do not run aimlessly, nor do I box as though beating the air; *but I punish my body and enslave it,* so that after proclaiming to others I myself should not be disqualified. (1 Cor. 9:24–27, emphasis added)

Fasting as body discipline has found a strong advocate today, if not a significant renewal, through the many writings of Dallas Willard. He has long advocated that we should return not only to the teachings but also the practices of Jesus and Paul. He also advocates that disciplining the body as did both Jesus and Paul will generate a more robust spiritual life for us today.[5] Willard makes an important point: "The unrestrained hedonism of our own day comes historically from the 18th-century idealization of happiness and is filtered through the 19th-century English ideology of pleasure as *the* good for people. Finally it emerges in the form of our present 'feel good' society."[6] Nothing could be more contrary to body discipline than these developments in history.

This yearning for pleasure and happiness, Willard reminds us, is not Paul's: he lived in a world where it was unthinkable to make progress morally or socially without training. Fasting fit into Paul's world as an element of spiritual discipline. Willard then famously contends, like the prayer from the Book of Common Prayer quoted earlier, that we have an inner and an outer dimension. But, and this needs renewed emphasis today, everything occurs through and in the *body*. If the body won't do what the spirit knows is good and right, then the body must be brought in line. And bringing the body back in line with the moral life is what Paul's statements affirm. Therefore, we find in the apostle Paul an early indicator of body discipline. One might say that if you discipline the body, the spirit will follow.

Here is where we have a tendency to take a misstep. Many of us are tempted to fast in order to get something—forgiveness or an answer for our prayers (the B ➜ C issue). Body discipline is not about the immediate resolution; instead, body discipline prepares a Christian for the long haul. This kind of discipline, like all the other kinds of fasting described in this volume, brings to expression an overall yearning to be more holy, to be more loving, and to be more responsive to God, self, others, and the entire world. Instead of marking down an urgent need and an immediate answer and fasting intensely for answers to those needs, body discipline engages the whole life in order to effect moral and spiritual development in one's sacred journey. Progress is measured in decades, not days.

Written into the fabric of this spiritual discipline is the grievous sacred moment, and we need once again to bring it to the surface. Read the last few sentences of the previous paragraph, or read carefully between the lines of Dallas Willard's or Adalbert de Vogüé's books, and you will see the grievous sacred moment generating the response of fasting. And what is it? The sacred moment of realizing our need to grow in grace, to shed sins, and to become more loving and holy. Body discipline, though, moves this from a spontaneous action to the world of daily responses to an ongoing mortal, moral condition.

The need for steady progress is why the Christian life, Paul claimed, may be compared to an athlete's life of discipline. He wrote, "Athletes exercise self-control in all things" (1 Cor. 9:25).

Our son, Lukas, played minor-league baseball for five seasons. The level of discipline, which brings its own sense of fulfillment and connects the athlete to other similarly disciplined athletes, astonished us at times. Diet, weight lifting, running, stretching, mental preparation, fastidious attention to details and to clothing and to shoes, not to mention relentless comparison to the opposition, all factor into the athlete's lifestyle we grew accustomed to as Lukas grew into his career as a player.

If the contemporary obsession with sports differs from the Roman Empire's and Paul's own world, it does so only in details—the Greeks and Romans unabashedly delighted in sporting events and competitions. Pindar penned his still-fun-to-read *The Odes* about athletic competitions; education occurred in a "gymnasium" (roughly "naked men wrestling place"); the marathon and decathlon arose into prominence prior to Paul; combat sports attracted thousands, and opponents sometimes collapsed into death before jeering and cheering fans. Archaeologists have discovered abundant evidence of the centrality of athletic events for the ancient world.[7] Like a chaplain speaking to professional football players prior to a game, Paul can perceive the entire Christian life in terms of the discipline of athletics. In 1 Timothy 4:7, he says, "Train [*gymnaze*] yourself in godliness." In fact, he elevates spiritual-athletic training over physical-athletic training: "for, while physical training [*somatike gymnasia*] is of some value, godliness [*eusebia*] is valuable in every way, holding promise for both the present life and the life to come" (v. 8).

No wonder, then, that Christians eventually reshape fasting into the full-blown practice of body discipline. Paul is an advocate for a total person (body and soul) battling with desire in order to "present your members to God" (Rom. 6:13), and he urges fellow Christians to "put to death . . . whatever in you is earthly: fornication, impurity, passion, evil desire, and greed (which is idolatry)" (Col. 3:5). Nothing can be clearer than Galatians 5:24: "Those who belong to Christ Jesus have crucified the flesh with its passions and desires" or "if by the Spirit you put to death the deeds of the body, you will live" (Rom. 8:13). Paul saw the Christian life as body discipline, and Dallas Willard contends that Paul's battle was victorious in part because of Paul's developing spiritual disciplines like fasting.

Willard is probably right. But we have to be fair with what the Bible says and doesn't say. In spite of Willard's enthusiasm for the disciplines as the embodied training ground for growth in spirituality, one must observe that Paul does not explicitly connect his statement about beating the body to fasting. In the book of Acts, it is said that Paul fasted at his conversion (9:9) and that he participated in group fasting to gain guidance from God (13:2–3; 14:23). But only twice did Paul himself address anything that can be understood today as disciplinary fasting. Here are the two references:

> As servants of God we have commended ourselves in every
> way: through great endurance, in *afflictions*, hardships,

> calamities, beatings, imprisonments, riots, labors, sleepless
> nights, *hunger*. (2 Cor. 6:4–5, emphasis added)

> In toil and hardship, through many a sleepless night, *hungry*
> *and thirsty, often without food*, cold and naked. (2 Cor. 11:27,
> emphasis added)

Most readers of these two passages ask the same questions:
Is this fasting or persecution? Is someone else depriving Paul of
food and water, or is this Paul's own discipline? The evidence, in
my judgment, is not clear. But in light of Paul's comparison of
ongoing moral development to athletic discipline, it is quite likely
that Paul was an early proponent of fasting as body discipline.

Paul, then, is probably an advocate for fasting regularly in
order to grow spiritually. But there is another source for the
most common form of fasting in the Christian world today.

ROUTINE BODY DISCIPLINE

Body discipline emerges from "stationary fasts"—that is, the routine scheduling of a day or two per week wherein the Christian
fasts from one evening meal to the next evening meal, or from
dinner one evening to midafternoon the next day, skipping food
(or even water) during the heat of the day. The logic of this
defense of body discipline is simple: the pious of Judaism fasted

twice a week; Jesus and his followers were pious; therefore, they also fasted twice a week. Life rarely reduces to logic, but in this case life probably does. I offer a brief defense of body discipline deriving from the time of Jesus.

Picking on a stereotype of pious hypocrisy, Jesus said that a Pharisee once went up to the temple to pray and said this: "God, I thank you that I am not like other people: thieves, rogues, adulterers, or even like this tax collector. *I fast twice a week*; I give a tenth of all my income" (Luke 18:11–12; emphasis added). Jesus' stereotyped pious Pharisee fasted twice a week, and we know from other sources that such a stationary fast became definitive for Jews. Jesus, we perhaps need to remind ourselves, was no more against fasting than he was against tithing—he was against the arrogant self-righteousness of a man who did the right things but whose heart remained pompous before God. If the pious Jew fasted twice a week, it is possible that Jesus and his followers did too—at least for some of their time together.

In contrast to the stereotyped hypocrisy Jesus put on public display in his parable, a good example of a pious Jew who fasted is Anna, the companion of Simeon in the temple, who camped out at the temple, waiting for God to bring justice for the poor. Notice that her fasting was a response to God's delayed ushering in of the kingdom of God. Luke tells us this about Anna: "She never left the temple but worshiped there with *fasting* and prayer night and day" (Luke 2:37, emphasis added). This woman seemed to fast daily—that is, she did not eat or drink from breakfast to the evening meal, or maybe she was like de Vogüé and fasted every day from the evening dinner to the next evening dinner. The scheduled practice of fasting is what I am calling *body discipline.*

Even more to the point of showing that the followers of Jesus fasted, the contemporaries of Jesus were surprised Jesus and his disciples *did not* fast (Mark 2:18–22). "Why," he was asked, "do John's disciples and the disciples of the Pharisees fast, but your disciples do not fast?" (v. 18). We'll get to this "eschatological fasting" in chapter 10, but for now we need to observe that fasting was so customary to Jewish piety that Jesus' nonfasting was a cause of surprise. Jesus, we can safely infer, clearly suspended fasting, but only *while he was present with his Messianic community.* Most notably, *after* his being "taken away from them" then, Jesus predicted, his disciples would resume the stationary fasting of his Jewish world (v. 20).

And that is exactly what we do find, though the record for it is found in an early Christian book not included in the New Testament. The famous line can be found in Didache 8:1: "But do not let your fasts coincide with those of the hypocrites. They fast on Monday and Thursday, so you must fast on Wednesday and Friday." Even if the motivation of the writer emerges from the desire to mark a clear boundary between Jews and the early Christians, the evidence is clear that many early Christians practiced a stationary fast on Wednesday and Friday. They ate breakfast, fasted from food (and perhaps water) during the day, and then broke that fast at the evening meal. It is also possible that they ate dinner and fasted until midafternoon the next day. Body discipline, then, derives from the time of Jesus.

That the early Christians fasted seems certain. *Why* they did so is not clear, and we should be careful not to impose our motives on them. Did they fast to further their moral development? To do battle with sins and desires? To create funds and supplies for the poor? To spend time in prayer pleading with God? Did they see some people as soldiers for the Lord whose fasting protected the community the way soldiers at their stations protected the community? Probably yes to each of these— and yet the honest student will admit that we don't really know why the early Christians practiced the stationary fast.

Even if we cannot always discern why the earliest Christians fasted, we can be confident that some grievous sacred moment prompted the fasting. In light of the themes we've already discussed, it is reasonable to think that body discipline was a response to the presence of sin, to the reality of a broken world, and to the yearning for holiness and love.

CHURCH TRADITION UNFOLDS BODY DISCIPLINE

I believe body discipline is a legitimate development of biblical and early Christian practice and belief. But I believe there is potential here for body discipline to become a dangerous exaggeration.[8] It all has to do with body image: as long as the person is seen holistically—body and soul—and as long as fasting is a response to a grievous sacred moment, Christian developments of fasting will be healthy. Yet the minute the body becomes the temporary location of evil desire, fasting can easily become unhealthy.

To illustrate the danger I am speaking of, we can look at a clear example. Simeon the Stylite wanted to pass the entire Lenten season of at least forty days without eating, and his willpower was sufficient to lead him through years of disciplined endeavor to where he could go a whole Lent without eating anything. Eventually he tied himself up so he could remain erect and then achieved the capacity to remain erect in prayer in his own strength. It was, as Adalbert de Vogüé described Simeon, "a magnificent conquest of self."[9] Indeed. But hardly important or necessary and certainly not worthy of emulation. One must ask if this is not more a potent illustration of willpower than an example of genuine development in spirituality.

MODERATION

The Christian practice of fasting on Wednesday and Friday naturally unfolded into a self-conscious Christian act of disciplining the body's desires so the whole person could live the life God intends. The body was not seen as a monster. Instead, sinful desires needed to be restrained, and there was no better way for this than to develop the habit of telling them no. One of the most widely read fasting books is Arthur Wallis's *God's Chosen Fast*. He states our point so well: "We do not need to extinguish the fire in the grate; only to prevent the coals from falling out and setting the place on fire."[10] The healthy side of the early Christian development was the moderate disciplinary fast designed to keep the coals of desire—mostly sexual, but also gluttonous—from falling out and setting the entire Christian on fire.

CELIBACY AND SUBDUING SEXUAL DESIRES

With the rise of celibacy as the ideal Christian life—and this book will not dip into this most controverted of developments—came disciplinary fasting as the dominant means of subduing sexual desire. Whenever celibacy is idealized, there is always the possibility for body image to freeze in the arctic tundra. Medical studies today prove that if you starve yourself long enough, or to put this more religiously, if you fast rigorously enough, sexual desire will be emphatically reduced—along with other desires, many of them as healthy as the desire for sexual relations.

St. Anthony of Egypt, the prototype ascetic monk, famously ate very little. Inspired by his example, Christians all over the early Christian world began to experiment more and more with radical fasting, and some of it was fueled by unhealthy, unChristian

perceptions of the body. Here is but one example: "I call as witnesses Jesus and his angels," the towering early Christian figure
Jerome once wrote in his *Life of Paul, the First Hermit*, "that . . . I
saw monks: one lived as a recluse for thirty years on coarse barley bread and muddy water; another subsisted on five dried figs
a day. . . . These things will seem unbelievable to those who do
not believe that all things are possible for those who believe."[11]
Radical fasting became the ideal for many; no one needs
to read between the lines to know that anorexia nervosa and
self-starvation followed easily from these ideals. St. Catherine
of Siena and St. Francis—it is frequently observed—all but
starved themselves to death. They were not alone.

Radical fasting became particularly connected to women,
and this occurred in part because males found females seduc-
tive. In words that haunted women and in part reshaped body
image for women, the often-extreme Jerome once spoke of the
ideal woman in these terms: "one who mourned and fasted,
who was squalid with dirt, almost blinded by weeping . . . The
psalms were her music, the Gospels her conversation, conti-
nence her luxury, her life a fast. *No other [woman] could give me
pleasure but one whom I never saw eating food*."[12] My wife is a psycholo-
gist who has seen more than her fair share of women with self-
starvation problems; I teach college students and have had,
sadly, a few students suffer from and even starve themselves to
death because of anorexia nervosa. When I hear words like
those of Jerome about radical fasting, I see a matter of life and

death, not just some religious discipline. These ideals can easily become dangerous.

PROBLEM: BODY DISCIPLINE
BECOMES BODY BATTLE

I have no debate with the need for each of us to battle lust, greed, pride, power, and other dehumanizing desires. Mohandas Gandhi, after fasting with others in order to develop self-restraint, said this: "For my part, however, I am convinced I greatly benefited by it both physically and morally."[13] Fasting can lead from the B column of response to the C column of results. My concern is this: the Bible shows almost no interest in fasting as a means to conquer the monster—that is, as a means for the spirit to overcome the passions or the soul to outlast the flesh in fight-till-you-die battle. For many, fasting is about the battle against the body. In our terms, it is only about B → C, about fasting as *instrumental* so that we fast in order to get something out of it. Let me put this more starkly now: fasting for some moves well beyond body discipline to become body battle. Unfortunately, because we have too often forgotten that fasting is a response to a sacred moment, body battle sometimes takes center stage.

One reason the church knows about body discipline (or body battle) is because of St. Anthony, whose life was memorialized in St. Athanasius's biography.[14] As St. Athanasius said of

Anthony, "It was a dictum of his that the soul's energy thrives when the body's desires are feeblest." After twenty years of ascetic solitude, Anthony emerged into society and "the state of his soul was pure . . . [for he] had himself completely under control—a man guided by reason and stable in his character." In a nutshell, this is body battle: conquer the body's desires through austere discipline, including fasting, and holiness follows.

Fasting as a means to conquer our monstrous desires—or, having conquered them, to keep them in check—seems inevitably tied to a disunity of body and spirit. The entire ascetic tradition finds its roots in body discipline fasting, but all of its extravagances emerge from the frequent distortion of the sacred unity of the person into an unhealthy dualism. Summarizing Anthony's entire approach, St. Athanasius recorded what I consider an unhealthy dualism about Anthony: "When he was about to eat and sleep and provide for the other needs of the body, shame overcame him as he thought of the spiritual nature of the soul," and that the spirit "must not be dragged down by the pleasures of the body, but rather the body must be made subject to the soul."

This is not to say that there aren't salutary virtues in body discipline fasting; to deny such is foolish. Who has not read of St. Anthony and received some benefit from his austere example? As St. Athanasius put it, "This man who lived hidden in a mountain was heard of in Spain and Gaul, in Rome and in Africa." Regardless of the fame and influence of those like Anthony, we offer up these two warnings: First, that body discipline must think more directly of the sacred moment that prompts it; second, that body discipline not lead to an all-out war between spirit and body that becomes body battle.

SOLUTION: BODY DISCIPLINE, NOT BODY BATTLE

Disciplinary fasting develops latent themes in the Bible. No one questions the importance of holding sinful desires in check. It is never right for a man or woman to engage in sexual intercourse with someone else's spouse. Holding back such desires is good Christian discipline. If one's stationary fast seeks to remind oneself of the need to maintain constant watch over one's moral life, then all to the good. Anchoring body discipline into a grievous sacred moment is important. In fact, body discipline seeks to make that sacred moment an ongoing life of struggling with sin and growing in holiness and love. This is all very good.

But Christians have had within them unhealthy perceptions of both sexuality and food. When sexual desire becomes evil or when food becomes a despised necessity, the Christian practice of disciplinary fasting can easily cascade into treating legitimate desire as a monster, and the body quickly becomes "bad." We need at times to remind ourselves that the Song of Solomon, a book rich with sexual imagery, is in the Bible, and that Jesus, unlike his older relative John the Baptist, was known for "eating and drinking" (Matt. 11:16–19). If the Bible can explain God's relationship to his people as ravishing sexuality (Hos. 1–3) and eternity as a feast with food and wine in abundance, then we need to remind ourselves of the goodness of our sexuality and dining—even if we will also sometimes need to check both inappropriate sex and gluttony by fasting.

7

FASTING AS
BODY CALENDAR

THE GREAT PREACHER JOHN WESLEY MADE AN OBSERVA-
tion about fasting that reminds of how customary fasting was in
a former era: "While we were at Oxford the rule of every
Methodist was (unless in case of sickness) to fast every Wednesday
and Friday in the year, in imitation of the primitive church, for
which they had the highest reverence."[1] But fasting among the
Methodists began to shift noticeably even as Wesley aged.

> And I fear there are now thousands of Methodists, so called,
> both in England and Ireland, who, following the same bad
> example, have entirely left off fasting; who are so far from
> fasting twice a week (as all the stricter Pharisees did) that
> they do not fast twice in the month. Yea, are there not some
> of you who do not fast one day, from the beginning of the
> year to the end?

And he cut the Methodists of his day no slack because fasting was for Wesley symbolic of spirituality itself: "Since, according to this, the man that never fasts is no more in the way to heaven than the man that never prays."[2]

Whatever you think of Wesley's dire warning, you cannot deny that times have surely changed. Perhaps Wesley was swept into a zeal for holiness, prayer, and fasting along with enough others that he could overstate his point. Probably so. But I know few places in the Western church today where one could ever contend that fasting is the mark of genuine spirituality.

WHAT HAPPENED?

The twenty-first century's lack of interest in fasting is not just the social drift away from rituals. The issue involves our body perceptions and the role the body plays in our spirituality. But there are other factors at work as well that have led the vast majority of Christians away from not only the practice of fasting but the entire church calendar.[3] Robert Webber, in one of the last books he wrote before pancreatic cancer took him from us, loved the church calendar and knew its formative powers. "Worship does God's story!" he boldly exclaimed in *Ancient-Future Worship*,[4] which is to say, genuine Christian worship lives out year by year by following the church calendar, the story of God's redemptive ways. If we annually follow that story, we will encounter the vital fasts that respond properly to that story.

But since the sixteenth century, Reformation Protestants have progressively dissociated themselves from Roman Catholics (and to a lesser degree the Eastern Orthodox) with their calendar. High-church Protestants, like Anglo-Catholics, have of course not done this as much as have low-church Protestants (like Baptists and various nondenominational Christians), but I know this: my own church tradition has *never* participated in any of the classical calendrical fasts of the Christian church. (Most of the church calendar has also been wiped away—we only celebrated Christmas [not Advent] and Holy Week [also called Good Friday and Easter].)

In many of our Western churches, the sacred fasts of the Christian tradition are never mentioned. Truth be told, we don't even know what they are. We do not fast on Wednesdays and Fridays, or on either day, as a routine; we never think about fasting on Saturday (to prepare for the Sabbath); we do not fast before Communion or before baptism. Well, yes, we do know what Lent is, but many evangelicals consider it something that Catholics do and therefore something we don't need to do because we have been saved from rituals. The widespread erasure of everything calendrical also erases the significance of memory in Christian worship. Most significantly, we don't read through the Scriptures aloud together as the liturgical churches have always done. Why? Again, the answer is simple: the calendar is Catholic; therefore, we don't do it. That erasure brings the heavy depression that comes from cutting out three-quarters of the history of the church from our memory.

What stopped me in my tracks about this erasure of the church calendar, with its dynamic creation of sacred rhythms, was the study of Jesus' prayer life. That study led to my book *Praying with the Church,* which has subsequently led me even further into the value of the church calendar, which in turn reveals an entire history of fasting.[5] What solidly clinches the need for Christians to participate in the church calendar is that *God prescribed a calendar for Israel*—and if God thought it was good for Israel, it just might be a good thing for the church. The reason the earliest Christians didn't reveal a newly minted church calendar is obvious: they were still using the Jewish calendar. Inherent to the Jewish calendar were annual fasts.

Once again, we need to return to the A → B → C pattern of fasting: sacred moment, response of fasting, and results. In Israel's ancient calendar, fasting was a response to two primary features: the sacredness of Israel's national life and the sacredness of a holy life. So sacred were these two that God revealed to Israel in its Torah that fasting was an annual event. Christians, too, followed this practice of annual fasts—what I call *body calendar*—and they were responding to similar features: the sacredness of the church's life and the sacredness of a holy life. Body calendar, then, is not simply an instrumental act but a profound, structured, annual response to corporate and personal life. The "calendar evoked that corporate and personal life and prompted Christians to respond to that sacredness with fasting.

We turn now to five features of the early Christian body calendar, and we must remind ourselves that these features were by and large maintained by the church (of all sorts) until the nineteenth or twentieth century. We might consider how we can bring these back into church life today.

STATIONARY FASTS: WEDNESDAY AND FRIDAY

The most notable feature, as we mentioned in our previous chapter, of ancient Christian practice—at least prior to the Reformation—was that all Christians (health issues aside) were expected to fast every Wednesday and Friday (with minor exceptions on feast days) and, with proper exceptions granted, every Christian seemingly did. This kind of fast is usually called "stationary" fasting. The word *station* comes from the Latin *statio*, a military term for a cohort, and suggests a communal commitment or resolve not to eat. The essence of this fast, then, is that it is a *group* fast. The church comes together to fast. The stationary fast, then, referred to days on which Christians did not eat either until noon, three o'clock in the afternoon, or even until dusk (the time of Vespers).

Fasting twice a week in our world is seen by many as excessive. Yet I wonder if we might reconsider bringing back a stationary fast in some creative ways. Perhaps Christians could fast from breakfast to dinner once or twice a week and do this for a month. Since I would discourage the desire to turn fasting into something instrumental, into something we use to get something we want, I also recommend that we restore stationary fasting to the church calendar and use each day of fasting to concentrate on the major events. Fasting can be seen as a response to those events in the life of Jesus. Or perhaps we devote a day each week to pray our way through major issues in our country and our world—such as poverty, environment, justice, economy, international strife, and so on. Both the major events in Jesus' life and the global crises that face us today are grievous sacred moments that surely can legitimately prompt fasting on our part.

Let's look briefly at three features of the stationary fast: it was not new, Christians were very serious about how they fasted, and they adapted the Jewish practice to make it more Christian.

THE ANCIENT CUSTOM OF STATIONARY FASTING

The origins of Christian stationary fasting are both Jewish custom and Jesus' practice. Jewish custom was to fast every Monday and Thursday—roughly from sunup to sundown or perhaps from the evening meal on one day to the noonday or evening meal the next day. Jesus assumed this practice for his followers on two occasions: in the Sermon on the Mount, when he informed his followers that their fasting habits were not to be ones that attracted attention to themselves (Matt. 6:16–18), and when he predicted that after he was taken back to God his followers would resume their regular fasting (Mark 2:18–22). In both of these instances, what Jesus no doubt had in mind was the stationary fast rather than a spontaneous fast to express repentance, grief, or supplication.

FASTING WITH RIGOR

John Cassian's name is inseparable from the word *rigor* and the great ascetic tradition of the church. When Bishop Castor of Apt (southeastern France) asked for advice on how the devoted ought to live, Cassian wrote his famous *Institutes*, a set of teachings that influenced the famous *Rule of Saint Benedict* and therefore shaped Western and Eastern spirituality. In Cassian's *Institutes*, he illustrated how rigorous some Christians were about fasting:

> A monk therefore who wants to proceed to the struggle of interior conflicts [body discipline] should lay down this as a precaution for himself to begin with: viz. : that he will not in any case allow himself to be overcome by any delicacies [sweet, savory, and rich foods], or take anything to eat or drink before the fast [statio] is over and the proper hour for refreshment has come, outside meal times; nor, when the meal is over, will he allow himself to take a morsel however small.[6]

The monkish ideal filtered into the practice of the laity: fasting was serious, and monks were expected to obey it fastidiously.

CHRISTIANIZING FASTING

The early Christians distanced themselves from their Jewish neighbors by fasting on different days (Wednesday and Friday instead of Monday and Thursday). Eventually, the Christians explained their choice of days theologically. Peter of Alexandria, who was beheaded for his faith by Maximin on November 24, AD 311, offers the customary early Christian explanation: "No one shall find fault with us for observing the fourth day of the week [Wednesday], and the preparation [Friday], on which it is reasonably enjoined us to fast according to the tradition. On the fourth day, indeed, because on it the Jews took counsel for the betrayal of our Lord; and on the sixth, because on it He himself suffered for us."[7] Christians fasted on Wednesday because Jesus suffered the betrayal and they participate in his suffering by fasting; they fasted on Friday as a response to Jesus' own suffering.

Stationary fasting became the custom of the church. John Wesley, in his *Journal*, wrote on Friday, August 17, 1739, that "many of our society met, as we had appointed, at one in the afternoon and agreed that all members of our society should obey the Church to which we belong by observing 'all Fridays in the year' as 'days of fasting and abstinence.' We likewise agreed that as many as had opportunity should then meet to spend an hour together in prayer."[8] Wesley was about twenty-five years old when he wrote this; he practiced fasting the rest of his life.

NOT ON THE SABBATH OR THE LORD'S DAY

There is a time to fast and a time not to fast. The two times not to fast are on the Sabbath and on the Lord's Day. Why? Because "the former is the memorial of the creation, and the latter of the resurrection."[9] Christians did make an exception about Sabbath fasting: they fasted on the Saturday (Sabbath) following Good Friday since on that day the Lord was "under the earth." It was the only Sabbath (the Great Sabbath) on which the Christians were not to feast.

Tertullian is one of the church's earliest and greatest apologists; he died in about AD 220. He expresses a common belief and practice when he says that "we count fasting or kneeling in worship on the Lord's day to be unlawful."[10] Why? They are behaviors out of sync with the joy of the day on which the resurrection of Jesus is celebrated. But Jerome, ever vigilant in ascetic practices and never afraid to go too far, once complained that he wished he could fast on the Lord's Day.[11] Jerome's yearning only proves how important not fasting on the Lord's Day was for the early Christians.

How serious were they about these things? From another early Christian book, *Constitutions of the Holy Apostles*, canon (rule) 64, we get this ruling: "If any one of the clergy be found to fast on the Lord's day, or on the Sabbath-day, excepting one only [Great Sabbath], let him be deprived; but if he be one of the laity, let him be suspended."[12] And from the Council of Gangra (held in the fourth century), we get this ruling: "If any one, under pretense of asceticism, shall fast on Sunday, let him be anathema [accursed]."[13]

Just in case you were wondering, they were very serious!

BEFORE THE LORD'S SUPPER

This early Christian custom of body calendar fasting is worthy of our imitation today. Throughout much of the history of the church, Christians were in a fasting condition when they took of the Lord's Supper, and that meal officially broke their fast. Why? Because as Israelites prepared for the Day of Atonement by fasting, so Christians prepared for the Lord's body and blood by fasting. In essence, the fast prior to the Lord's Supper—beginning after the evening meal or that morning—was a fast in response to and repentance from one's sins. It prepared the Christian for the atoning power of Christ's death represented in the eating and drinking of the body and blood.

This led them to discuss the best time of day to serve the Eucharist. St. Augustine, the most influential voice of the Western church in the first millennium, urged leaders to offer the Lord's Supper prior to the ninth hour (approximately 3 p.m.) so that all those who were fasting would not have to break their fast prior to the Eucharist. "Wherefore we neither compel nor do we dare to forbid any one to break his fast before the Lord's

Supper on that day."[14] John Wesley spoke of the same practice in the eighteenth century: "Now it is well known there is always a fast-day in the week preceding the administration of the Lord's Supper." And he then proceeds in the sermon to ridicule the Church of Scotland for delicate meals on the fast day![15]

Skipping breakfast on a Sunday morning prior to Eucharist is not outside the limits for most of us. Eucharistic fasting responds to our consciousness of sin and to contemplation on the suffering of Jesus Christ, both of which are profound sacred moments.

BEFORE BAPTISM

Within a century, the Christian church practiced infant baptism, and therefore only converts to the faith were asked to fast prior to their baptism. Body calendar shaped the conversion process itself.

We saw earlier that the apostle Paul fasted at his conversion (Acts 9:9), and I suggested that we might reconsider his practice today. One reason to reconsider this practice is that the church regularly advocated fasting prior to baptism—assuming, of course, the baptism of an adult after conversion and catechism. The *Recognitions of Clement*, a didactic novel about Clement's encounter with the apostle Peter, reflects the Christian practices of some Christians in the third century AD, and most notably there is a clear assumption of the need to fast prior to baptism.

When Niceta requests baptism from Peter, he says, "But she must fast at least one day first, and so be baptized."[16]

LENT

Lent, for those who have grown up with the practice, is a time to give up something as an act of abstinence. Friends of mine usually speak of giving up chocolate or desserts or TV or sports or dining out. Most find something that they are either too committed to or that is unhealthy, and it therefore costs them something. This reminds them of what Jesus gave up.

These acts of abstinence are modern innovations on a rich, deep, and costly practice of fasting for forty days prior to Easter. The church did not practice the forty-day fast up to Lent immediately, but within a few centuries the custom was "catholic"—all churches everywhere observed the Lenten fast. To be sure, the length of the fast varied—in Rome it was for three weeks; in the Eastern churches for seven weeks. The fast was rigorous in that only one meal was permitted per day and Christians were not permitted to eat flesh or white meats during Lent, though exceptions were made and the mealtime was sometimes placed earlier in the day. The fast ended for some at midnight of the Great Sabbath (the Saturday between Good Friday and Easter).

If the early Christians didn't always agree on the length and nature of the Lenten fast, what united the church from very early on was a commitment to use the forty days of Lent as a time of introspection, confession, penitence, and fasting to prepare for the miracle of forgiveness on Good Friday and its life-giving power on Easter. It was a time structured to respond to sin, to be purged of inordinate desires, to yearn for forgiveness, and to develop patterns of holy living. Body calendar fasting comes into its own during Lent.

St. Athanasius, a bishop of Alexandria who wielded an abiding influence on the faith Christians now confess, in his Easter letter in AD 334, wrote of the requirement of fasting by interpreting the wilderness wanderings of Israel for forty years as a type of the Christian experience during Lent:

> But as Israel, when going up to Jerusalem, was first purified in the wilderness, being trained to forget the customs of Egypt, the Word by this typifying to us *the holy fast of forty days*, let us first be purified and freed from defilement, so that when we depart hence, having been careful of fasting, we may be able to ascend to the upper chamber with the Lord, to sup with Him; and may be partakers of the joy which is in heaven. *In no other manner is it possible to go up to Jerusalem, and to eat the Passover, except by observing the fast of forty days.*[17]

Besides the forty days corresponding to the wilderness years of Israel, St. Augustine observed that Moses fasted for forty days, Elijah did too; and Jesus fasted for forty days and nights.

Moses is the Law, Elijah the prophets, and Jesus the gospel—the whole Bible testifies to a forty-day fast![18]

THE BOOK OF COMMON PRAYER

I believe we can learn much about the spiritual discipline of fasting from the Book of Common Prayer. Here is the opening for the Ash Wednesday service, the day that begins Lent and that reminds the worshipper of its central themes—sin, repentance, fasting, and the preparation for forgiveness.

Let us pray.

Almighty and everlasting God, you hate nothing you have made and forgive the sins of all who are penitent: Create and make in us new and contrite hearts, that we, worthily lamenting our sins and acknowledging our wickedness, may obtain of you, the God of all mercy, perfect remission and forgiveness; through Jesus Christ our Lord, who lives and reigns with you and the Holy Spirit, one God, for ever and ever. Amen.

Old Testament Joel 2:1–2, 12–17; Isaiah 58:1–12

Psalm 103, or 103:8–14

Epistle 2 Corinthians 5:20b–6:10

Gospel Matthew 6:1–6, 16–21

After the Sermon, all stand, and the Celebrant or Minister appointed invites the people to the observance of a holy Lent, saying

Dear People of God: The first Christians observed with great devotion the days of our Lord's passion and resurrection, and it became the custom of the Church to prepare for them by a season of penitence and fasting. This season of Lent providesa time in which converts to the faith were prepared for Holy Baptism. It was also a time when those who, because of notorious sins, had been separated from the body of the faithful were reconciled by penitence and forgiveness, and restored to the fellowship of the Church. Thereby, the whole congregation was put in mind of the message of pardon and absolution set forth in the Gospel of our Savior, and of the need which all Christians continually have to renew their repentance and faith.

I invite you, therefore, in the name of the Church, to the observance of a holy Lent, by self-examination and repentance; by prayer, fasting, and self-denial; and by reading and meditating on God's holy Word. And, to make a right beginning of repentance, and as a mark of our mortal nature, let us now kneel before the Lord, our maker and redeemer.
Silence is then kept for a time, all kneeling.

If ashes are to be imposed, the Celebrant says the following prayer

Almighty God, you have created us out of the dust of the earth: Grant that these ashes may be to us a sign of our mortality and penitence, that we may remember that it is only by your gracious gift that we are given everlasting life; through Jesus Christ our Savior. Amen.

The ashes are imposed with the following words

Remember that you are dust, and to dust you shall return.

A SUMMARY

Israel fasted within the confines of a calendar alongside its spontaneous fasting to express repentance, supplication, and grief. A notable feature of Israel's fasting practices was the development of the spiritual discipline of stationary fasting— on Monday and Thursday. Jesus fasted, and he both assumed and predicted that his own followers would participate in the stationary fasting of Judaism. The early Christians fasted, and texts reveal that they practiced their own stationary fasting and distinguished themselves from their Jewish neighbors by doing so on Wednesdays and Fridays, and they explained their fasting as a kind of suffering with Christ in his betrayal and death. Within a few centuries, the entire Christian church learned to fast for forty days during Lent in order to prepare themselves for celebrating forgiveness, victory over sin, and the joy of life that explodes in Christian liturgy on Easter. Fasting featured prominently in the church's body calendar.

A SUGGESTION

In this chapter, I don't have room to explain even half of the fasting disciplines of the church, especially in the Eastern Orthodox tradition.[19] There are ember days and Rogation Days, and there are also vigils connected with other festivals.[20] Much of this is described in terms most Christians today don't even recognize. What we should perhaps ponder is where we are today in comparison with the generations who have gone before us. To be sure, there are dangers whenever religious disciplines are legislated or brought back into play simply because the church used to do it this way, but Christians receive Scripture as God's Word—and the God of that Word is the one who legislated fasts for Israel. The church carried out that divine blueprint as it reshaped the church calendar into a new form that was entirely focused on the life of Jesus Christ. Who are we to neglect what God's people have always done?

Let the last word be Martin Luther's. In his famous commentary on the Sermon on the Mount, this hot-penned Reformer weighs in on the fasting practices of the Catholic leaders of his day—and when Luther weighs in, the floor gives!

In typical bombastic fashion, he excoriates the hypocrisy of the "papists." After warning everyone left and right, Luther then commends two kinds of fasting for Christians: a civil fast and some calendrical fasts. The civil fast is ordered by the government and is clearly instrumental in Luther's ideas: "for one or two days a week there should be no eating or selling of meat. This would be a good and useful ordinance for the country, so that everything is not gobbled up as it is now, until finally hard times come and nothing is available." All of this is "to teach people to live a little more moderately." Then he commends fasting before Easter, before Pentecost, and before Christmas as "an outward Christian discipline and exercise for the young and simple people, by which they can learn to keep track of the seasons and to make the proper distinctions throughout the year." And, he adds, "I would be willing to condone fasts on every Friday evening throughout the year."[21]

No one feared the danger of ritual more than Luther, and he exhorted his followers to a body calendar—fasting on Friday nights and at three seasons of the year. I end this chapter with a challenge: should not many of us reconsider the body calendar of the Bible and the church?

8

FASTING AS
BODY POVERTY

EVERY RELIGIOUS TRADITION FINDS A WAY TO IDENTIFY core practices as "covenant path markers"[1]—practices that demonstrate to God, to the individual conscience, and to the world that someone is pious and approved by the community. Covenant path markers expose the faithful path on the covenant journey. Some churches focus on social justice, others on evangelism, others on Bible knowledge, others on church attendance, others on not having sex before they get married, and yet others on liturgical practices. I've never encountered any Christian groups for whom fasting was the covenant path marker. But the prophet Isaiah found himself in a community that saw fasting as the sure covenant path marker (Isa. 58). What the prophet said to his audience, ironically, threatened the viability of fasting as a spiritual discipline.

Here's the prophet Isaiah's famous line: "Is not this the fast that I choose: to loose the bonds of injustice?" (58:6). It sure seems at first blush that Isaiah is out to redefine "fast" from "food abstinence" to "working for social justice." *Au contraire*! To ask if fasting is replaced by social-justice work misses the point of the passage. Isaiah's trenchant comments target pious Israelites who *were* fasting and were complaining that God was not answering their supplications. In other words, Isaiah criticized the instrumental approach to fasting and taught Israel to reconsider what fasting is all about. Isaiah's ideas can help us today to reformulate both what we think and how we practice fasting. Let's explore some of the ideas of Isaiah 58 about fasting, because this passage deserves more attention in our world today.

ISAIAH'S SACRED MOMENT: INJUSTICE IN THE COMMUNITY

Notice the stinging questions Isaiah asked of them:

> Is not this the fast that I choose:
>> to loose the bonds of injustice,
>> to undo the thongs of the yoke,
> to let the oppressed go free,
>> and to break every yoke?
> Is it not to share your bread with the hungry,
>> and bring the homeless poor into your house;
> when you see the naked, to cover them,
>> and not to hide yourself from your own kin? (vv. 6–7)

In our A → B → C approach to fasting, the A column for Isaiah is the *condition of the poor and the presence of injustice in one's own community*. To dig even deeper, Isaiah said fasting is a *response to God's response to the poor and to the presence of injustice*. The great Jewish writer Abraham Heschel explored the prophet's role in Israel as one of *pathos*—that is, of a prophet taking on God's very disposition with respect to Israel so much so that the prophet embodied God's Word to God's people. Fasting, one might say, is the faithful person's pathos for and with the poor— fasting embodies God's disposition to the poor.[2] Fasting, then, is body poverty in response to injustice in our world.

ISAIAH'S VISION: THE KINGDOM OF GOD AND JUSTICE

Isaiah wanted his audience to understand that fasting transcends the spirituality of the individual. (This is something we especially need to hear if we are given to the instrumental view of fasting and wondering what we will get out of it.) Body poverty is an act of faith and hope for others. Notice the opening words of the third division of Isaiah's prophecies at the onset of chapter 56: "Thus says the LORD: Maintain justice [*mishpat*], and do what is right [*tsedeqa*], for soon my salvation [*yeshua*] will come, and my deliverance [*tsedeqa*] be revealed."[3] Body poverty reveals that establishing that kind of kingdom cannot be relegated to the king. It falls on the shoulders of everyone, together, to respond to the needs of others by divesting ourselves of some resources for the common good. When God's people look around and fail to see justice and righteousness and salvation and deliverance, and instead they see poverty and injustice, God's people should respond in body poverty.

ISAIAH'S PROBLEM: PERSONAL PIETY NULLIFIED BY OPPRESSION

The people of Isaiah's day yearned for a personal relation with God: "Day after day they seek me and delight to know my ways . . . they ask of me righteous judgments, they delight to draw near to God" (Isa. 58:2). In their personal spirituality they fast but are not getting through to God: "Why do we fast, but you do not see? Why humble ourselves, but you do not notice?" (v. 3). Here's why, Isaiah must reveal to them: "Look, you serve your own interest on your fast day, and oppress all your workers. Look, you fast only to quarrel and to fight and to strike with a wicked fist" (vv. 3–4). And the thunderous, James Earl Jones–like words echoed throughout the temple's walls: "Such fasting as you do today will not make your voice heard on high" (v. 4). Fasting that does not lead to consideration of the poverty of others misses the whole point.

Isaiah's contemporaries were noted by a pious, intense spirituality. But their personal, self-centered piety was not shaped by God's design of a just community. If you go in prayer to the God who wants to bring justice, then you should be willing to spend your energies working for that same justice. Isaiah's contemporaries consumed their piety on themselves; they saw no inconsistency between their self-consumptive piety and their oppression of their own workers, and their fasting seemingly led them to fight with one another. Selfishness, oppression, and contentiousness contradict justice, righteousness, and peace.

The zeal of God burned in Isaiah.

FASTING REDEFINED

Fasting, like a star in the sky, is only one star in the constellation of spirituality. As the priest and Levite thought they could follow the Torah and *not* offer aid to the stranded, dying man (Luke 10:25–37), so Isaiah's community thought they could abstain from food and pass by the needs of others on their way to God. Fasting never stands alone. Fasting, if it is genuine, brings us into a communal spirituality because it is a response to the lack of justice in the community. If the inner overwhelms the outer, a person's body image crumbles; and if private spirituality overwhelms the communal, a person's fasting vaporizes. That's Isaiah's point. Fasting is body poverty—self-impoverishment as a response to the impoverishment of others.

So Isaiah urges his listeners to commit themselves fully to God, and he redefines *fasting* for his listeners. What is fasting? According to Isaiah, it involves

- undoing injustice;
- releasing the oppressed;
- feeding the hungry;
- providing sanctuary for the homeless.

Isaiah was surrounded by people who fasted instrumentally—they wanted to know God more and to worship him more intensely. Isaiah summoned his audience to see that genuine fasting was a response to injustices in the land. And the proper response to that injustice was the kind of fast that not only got to know God, but also responded in compassion to the poor and in efforts to establish justice in the land and in zeal for peace among the people of God.

When we boil down Isaiah's great redefinition of fasting, we find that he believes fasting has two companions.

THE COMPANIONS OF FASTING

There are two companions to fasting, according to Isaiah 58. The first is that fasting be converted into justice and solidarity with others. The second is that fasting leads to holiness. The genuine fast then becomes body poverty—affliction of self for the good of others and the good of one's own moral life.

JUSTICE AND SOLIDARITY

The first companion of fasting is *to give to the poor,* or more generally, to pursue *justice.* What we give up in food when we fast can be converted to gifts to the poor; what we give up in time not spent eating can be converted into time spent relieving injustices. An early Christian writing that survives to this day, called *The Shepherd of Hermas,* gives advice both on fasting from sin and on converting the fast into charity. After refraining from bread and water, the Christian is to "estimate the cost of the food you would have eaten on that day and give that amount to a widow or orphan or someone in need. Be humble in this way, that the one who receives something because of your humility may fill his own soul and pray to the Lord for you."[4]

A few hundred years later, St. Augustine advised something similar, beginning with this: "Fasting chastens yourself: it does not refresh others. Your distress will profit you if you afford comfort to others." He continued with this question: "How many poor can be filled by the breakfast we have this day given up?"[5] On Friday, February 17, 1744, John Wesley and his friends observed a solemn fast. "In the afternoon, many being met together, I exhorted them . . . to deal their bread to the hungry, to clothe the naked, and not to hide themselves from their own flesh. And God opened their hearts, so that they contributed near fifty pounds, which I began laying out the very next hour, in linen, woolen, and shoes, for them whom I knew to be diligent and yet in want."[6]

Justice has a sibling called *solidarity*. Many today who fast for the poor do so in part as a way of forging solidarity with the poor. The starkness of the act makes solidarity fasting not unlike the prophetic actions of Israel's prophets. As Ahijah ripped his cloak into twelve pieces (1 Kings 11:29–30) or as Jeremiah broke a pot in front of an audience (Jer. 19:1–13) or as Isaiah walked about naked for three years (Isa. 20:1–6), so contemporaries starve in public in order to express their theology, their hope, and their protest. We can explain this theoretically as follows: food joins humans to other humans because we share meals together. Whenever we give up food intentionally, we refrain from relationships. When a group protests by fasting, they both negate one relationship—with the haves—and they affirm another relationship—with the have-nots. And since the structures of power always have sufficient food, fasting is not only refusing relationship, but it is also protesting the power structures that exist.[7] That's theory. Here are some real examples.

In 1994, Representative Tony Hall, a devout Christian and Ohio Democrat, fasted for twenty-two days. Then he summoned Christians to fast three days during Holy Week to "raise the consciousness of the nation. I want people to begin to realize there are 25 million Americans that are hungry, who go to food banks and soup kitchens, and half of them are under the age of 17."[8] When asked about the value of fasting, Tony Hall said this: "It is a way of taking the focus off yourself to put it on something else, a way to humble yourself before God."[9] Though he didn't put it in our terms, his idea of fasting was for people to become more aware of the sacred moment worthy of repentance: that grievous sacred moment is injustice and poverty in our country.

When the new millennium turned over, Christians were fasting to call attention to the poor and to demonstrate identification. A major leader in this movement was David Duncombe, whose story has been repeatedly told,[10] and Duncombe laid down this claim: "Until the burden of debt is lifted from the poor, I am morally constrained to stand with them in their hunger."[11] Duncombe's story involved a forty-five-day fast in the halls of Congress, during which time his seventy-one-year-old frame lost thirty-five pounds, his body temperature dropped to 94–96 degrees, his blood pressure descended to 85/60, and he could sleep only three to four hours per night. He was fasting to get Congress to pass HR 1095. He was responding to injustice. His fast eventually required a four-legged walker. Senator Joe Biden said this to Duncombe as his fast came to an end: "You have shown us how anyone can rise above personal interest and partisan politics and lead this country by putting ourselves at risk for the good of all." Duncombe's parting comment: "Because the one goal of this ministry was to help save thousands of lives each day from starvation, to risk death by starvation myself was a morally acceptable means to this end." The "Wednesday Night Miracle" eventually led both houses of Congress to pass the resolution, and the president signed a $435 million package of debt forgiveness that helped countries feed their own poor.

Eamon Duffy, a professor in church history in Cambridge (England), bemoans the vaporization of fasting in the Catholic Church. Not least among his reasons are its prophetic witness and public solidarity in distinction to private fasting: "There is a world of difference between a private devotional gesture, the action of the specially pious, and the prophetic witness of the whole community—the matter-of-fact witness, repeated week by week, that to be Christian is to stand among the needy."[12]

As an aside, you might ask, how do we square these overtly public acts of fasting with the clear warning of Jesus in the Sermon on the Mount to hide our time of fasting so that it is not known to others (Matt. 6:16–18)? Besides the obvious fact that somehow Jesus made known his own fasting prior to his temptations, the warning of Jesus is about motive—displaying our piety in order to gain glory for our piety—rather than actual practice. As long as our motive is not to seek glory from others, we can fast in a way that others might know.

HOLINESS

The second companion of fasting is to fast *from sin and bad habits*. The Ninevites, as described in the book of Jonah, received reprieve not because they fasted in sackcloth but because their fasting was genuine body turning (Jonah 3:5–10). As the famous early Christian preacher John Chrysostom once put it, "for the honor of fasting consists not in abstinence from food, but in with-drawing from sinful practices." He continues: "If you see a poor man, take pity on him! If you see an enemy, be reconciled to him! If you see a friend gaining honor, do not envy him!" And, "Do not let just your mouth fast, but also the eye and the ear and the feet and the hands and all the members of our bodies. Let the hands fast by being pure from theft and avarice. Let the feet fast by ceasing from running to the unlawful spectacles . . . Let the mouth fast as well from disgraceful speeches and railing." The point for Chrysostom was formative. When conversing with others about fasting during Lent, Chrysostom had this to say:

> It is common for every one to ask in Lent, how many weeks each has fasted; and some may be heard saying they have fasted two, others three, and others that they have fasted the whole of the weeks. But what advantage is it, if we have gone through the fast devoid of works? If another says, "I have fasted the whole of Lent," you should say, "I had an enemy, but I was reconciled; I had a custom of evil-speaking, but I put a stop to it; I had a custom of swearing, but I have broken through this evil practice.[13]

Chrysostom was responding to injustice and to personal sin, and that is why he had a full-orbed view of fasting.

Recently Lynne Baab, a writer on spiritual formation, de-voted a book to the theme of expanding our sense of fasting.

While I'm not in favor of her language, I do think her overall emphasis is sound. "Christian fasting," she contended, "is the voluntary denial *of something* for a specific time, for a spiritual purpose, by an individual, family, community or nation."[14] She talked about "fasting" from TV and from jewelry as well as from the news media, e-mail, shopping, novels, music, and driving the car. These "fasts" are meant simply to be denials of our pleasures and our habits in order to draw us closer to God. Fasting for her is about severing the lines toward dependencies that have become "needs," even though they are not strictly needed. I prefer to call these "abstinences," but I agree that the impact of severing ourselves from our wants and desires can provoke us unto a deeper holiness. Lynne Baab rightly sees that fasting is a response to something and is also an act to do something about it. It is, in some instances, then body poverty—poverty over the self's condition.

THE PROMISE

We will look at the benefits of fasting in chapter 9, but for now we can pause to observe that, through Isaiah, the Lord promised Israel that if they got their fasting in line with the overall constellation of a proper spirituality, that if their fasting was turned into body poverty instead of selfish consumption and the abuse of power, they would be blessed. Notice this poetic promise from Isaiah 58:

If you remove the yoke from among you,

> the pointing of the finger, the speaking of evil,

if you offer your food to the hungry

> and satisfy the needs of the afflicted,

then your light shall rise in the darkness

> and your gloom be like the noonday.

The LORD will guide you continually,

> and satisfy your needs in parched places,

> and make your bones strong;

and you shall be like a watered garden,

> like a spring of water,

> whose waters never fail.

Your ancient ruins shall be rebuilt;

> you shall raise up the foundations of many generations;

you shall be called the repairer of the breach,

> the restorer of streets to live in. (vv. 9–12)

As in Isaiah's world, so also in ours: nothing is automatic. Fasting is not some kind of magical manipulation of God. But if we, as God's people, will turn from selfish pursuits and the abuses of power to face the poor in our midst and strive for justice, justice will roll into our communities in ways never imagined. Fasting is connected to God and to God's vision. If we come to God with God's vision in mind and surrender our entire person—spirit and body—in body poverty for that vision, we just might discover that God's blessings will pour forth.

9

FASTING AS
BODY CONTACT

FIVE OF THE MOST SIGNIFICANT FIGURES IN THE BIBLE—
Moses, Elijah, Daniel, Jesus, and Paul—fasted and experienced
unusual intimacies with God. No one can dispute either of
these claims. Are they connected? Probably. Did they intentionally prepare themselves for an intimate encounter by purifying
themselves through fasting? There is no evidence for that in the
Bible. But Christians through the ages have connected the fasting of these five figures with their intimate encounters with
God. Not only have they made that connection, but they've
also concluded that one way to encounter God intimately is to
fast. The act of depriving the body from food and even water
can lead to special mystical experiences.

Phillip H. Wiebe's book *Visions of Jesus* reveals that fasting
is sometimes connected to visions and intimate moments with
God.[1] Whatever one thinks of this, Christians throughout the

ages have both prepared themselves for encounters with God through fasting and found themselves lifted into God's very presence while fasting. The experience of an encounter with God is so intense that it requires complete focus on God. In a nutshell, the theory at work often is this: by denying oneself the pleasures of food, one can achieve holiness, pure love, and union with God. Many in the history of the church, especially from the fourth to the sixteenth centuries, believed union with God was nearly impossible to achieve without rigorous fasting and solitude. So, in an effort to experience God more directly, many fasted intensely.

My own study of fasting and fasters leads me to frame the connection of fasting and intimate union with God in a different way. Once again, we think of the A → B → C pattern: sacred moment, response of fasting, and result. If B (fasting) leads to C (intimate encounter with God), that does not mean that B causes C. My own study reveals that it is A that prompts B and leads to C. In other words, *those who yearn for God the most often realize the superficiality of their intimacy with God, fast in response to that superficiality, and then (on the other side) find themselves entranced in the presence of the angels and God.*

Fasting is to union with God what a marriage ring is to a loving couple. As the ring is not what prompts their union, so also the fasting is not what prompts union with God. Love prompts the giving of a ring, and it is the love that moves the relationship beyond the ring to genuine union with one another. So I would say that a more complete view of fasting suggests that it is the combination of our yearning to know God and our present state of not knowing God intimately enough that prompts the person to fast with the hope of encountering God. The grievous sacred moment (A) is our lack of intimacy with God.

WISDOM OF THE AGES

John Cassian, one of the church's masters of spirituality, yearned for God and purity of heart: "We ought therefore to bestow attention on bodily abstinence that we may by this fasting attain to purity of heart." And then he created a ladder of perfection:

> For this [pure heart] we must seek for solitude, for this we know that we ought to submit to fastings, vigils, toils, bodily nakedness, reading, and all other virtues that through them we may be enabled to prepare our heart and to keep it unharmed by all evil passions, and resting on these steps to mount to the perfection of charity.

After saying fasting is a "secondary" matter, Cassian said, "We ought to practice with a view to our main object, i.e., purity of heart" and to "perfection" so that the "soul may cleave to God and to heavenly things."[2] Cassian's emphasis tilts toward the instrumental understanding of fasting—that it is a means to get something we want—but anyone familiar with his writing knows that *im*purity of heart and *non*intimacy with God prompted his yearnings for God and a pure heart.

MOSES, ELIJAH, DANIEL, JESUS, AND PAUL

So much for the wisdom of the ages. The Protestant impulse is this: can we find the idea of fasting as body contact in the Bible? I'd like to draw us back again to five central figures in the Bible—Moses, Elijah, Daniel, Jesus, and the apostle Paul—and observe that each was to one degree a mystic or received visions, and that each was known for rigorous fasting. Each reveals what can only be called a kind of fasting that leads to body contact with God.

MOSES

At the heart of the Abrahamic faiths is the remarkable story of Moses, who, apart from Jesus, encountered God more intimately than anyone in the Bible. Moses had a *conversation* with God. "Then Moses went up to God; the LORD called to him from the mountain," so the Bible says in the opening paragraph of Exodus 19 (v. 3). And then it says that "Moses would speak and God would answer him in thunder" (v. 19). A remarkable verse in the Bible is Exodus 33:11: "Thus the LORD used to speak to Moses face to face, as one speaks to a friend." Even more remarkably, Moses *saw* God: "Show me your glory [*kavod*], I pray," Moses asks God (33:18). God answered Moses' prayer and displayed his glory to Moses. Here are the Bible's words:

The LORD passed before him, and proclaimed,

"The LORD, the LORD,
a God merciful and gracious,
slow to anger,
and abounding in steadfast love and faithfulness,
keeping steadfast love for the thousandth generation,
forgiving iniquity and transgression and sin,
yet by no means clearing the guilty,
but visiting the iniquity of the parents
upon the children and the children's children,
to the third and the fourth generation."

And Moses quickly bowed his head toward the earth, and worshiped. He said, "If now I have found favor in your sight, O Lord, I pray, let the Lord go with us. Although this is a stiff-necked people, pardon our iniquity and our sin, and take us for your inheritance." (Ex. 34:6–9)

Why bring up this experience of Moses? Because prior to conversing with and seeing God, Moses *fasted*: "He was there with the LORD forty days and forty nights; he neither ate bread nor drank water. And he wrote on the tablets the words of the covenant, the ten commandments" (34:28). An extreme fast by all accounts, and most explain it as a supernatural fast, since it is impossible for a normal human being to go without water for more than a few days. As the Jewish scholar Nahum Sarna put it: "In this extrasensuous world he [Moses] transcends the constraints of time and is released from the demands of his physical being."[3] Fasting and the presence of God go together. What is not often mentioned in this context is the nature of the sacred moment. It was the numinous holiness of God, the awe and majesty of God's presence on the top of Mount Sinai that prompted—compelled—Moses to fast. So overwhelmed was Moses by being in the presence of God that he could not bear to think of eating or drinking.

God's presence is so sacred, humans respond naturally by fasting. Contemplation of God and worship of God frequently do the same. Because fasting and God's presence are connected, Jews recite the "thirteen attributes of God" (found in the text above from Exodus 34:6–9) on *fast days*.

ELIJAH

A similar story is told of Elijah in 1 Kings 19. Frightened to death by the threat of the wicked Jezebel, Elijah fled into the wilderness, sat under a solitary broom tree, and fell asleep—only to be awakened by an angel who told him to eat "a cake baked on hot stones, and [drink] a jar of water" (v. 6). After lying down for a while longer, the angel again urged him to eat and drink.

Elijah then was sustained by that mannalike provision for forty days and nights. Most importantly, following this fast, Elijah encountered God passing by him on the mountain.

DANIEL

Daniel, too, fasted and had intimate moments with God. Most notable for Daniel is that he "turned to the Lord God, to seek an answer by prayer and supplication with fasting and sackcloth and ashes" (Dan. 9:3). He was heard. But being heard is only part of it; Daniel received visions and answers to prayer as a result of his communion with God prepared for by fasting. Sometime later, after mourning for three weeks and observing the partial fast from delicacies, meat, wine, and anointing, Daniel had another vision (10:2–3).

JESUS

After fasting for forty days and nights, like Moses and Elijah—and Luke's gospel says Jesus "ate nothing at all during those days" (4:2)—Jesus was hungry. (No kidding!) Before he ate anything, Jesus was visited by "the devil" (v. 2) and tempted to eat by ending his fast prior to its appointed time, to assert his rightful control over all the kingdoms of this world prior to its appointed time, and to jump recklessly from the pinnacle of the temple apart from divine permission (Luke 4:1–13). Some consider even the temptations of Jesus part of a "vision" and generated in part by his famished condition brought on by fasting.

I have my doubts that Jesus' temptations were simply visions, and I doubt that the temptations were brought on from lack of food. Regardless, *fasting* is connected to a unique encounter with the devil, a special intimacy with God, and a public affirmation of that intimacy above everything else.

More slender is the connection frequently made between Jesus' so-called mountaintop experiences and fasting. At Jesus' baptism, we are told only that Jesus was "praying" (Luke 3:21) when he heard the voice of God. When Jesus was transfigured, Luke tells us that Jesus was in prayer when the luminous transfiguration occurred (9:29). In each of these events, we are told Jesus was in prayer. Nothing is said about fasting. Perhaps these sacred moments were prepared for by fasting. Perhaps not.

PAUL

The apostle Paul fasted, and he reveals that he was often physically weakened by afflictions (2 Cor. 6:4–5; 11:27). Just after Paul's mentioning that he had been weakened often through fasting, Paul speaks of himself in the third person. He "knows a person in Christ" who had been lifted from earth into "the third heaven." He heard things he was not permitted to repeat, but of these experiences he would not boast—instead, drawing us back again to his fasting, he would speak only of his weaknesses (12:1–10). I've made the connections here between Paul's visions and his fasting as tightly as I think possible—and probably a little tighter than the evidence permits—in order to make the case that the apostle Paul was both a faster and one who was drawn into intimate union and vision of God.

Even this brief sketch of these five figures shows that fasting and intimate union with God can be connected. It is important to emphasize that *we* are making this connection, that the texts do not explicitly say, "If you fast, you will experience God more deeply." What concerns me is that some Christians may convert simple texts into an instrumental view of fasting: that fasting somehow triggers union with God. Instead, the deeper biblical tradition reveals that sacred moments trigger the response of fasting that sometimes—but not always—leads to some desired result. What I see in these texts are sacred moments like the utter holiness of God, fear, a yearning to be more holy, and concern for God's kingdom and others that prompted these instances of fasting. Fasting is not simply a B ➜ C movement. Fasting is the natural response to a grievous sacred moment that makes eating sacrilegious.

Let's turn back now to the wisdom of the church, to St. Athanasius, Basil the Great, and John Calvin.

PREPARATION AND ENCOUNTER

In one of his letters, St. Athanasius, the great articulator of Trinitarian faith, declared that contemplating God will sustain us physically: "Let him believe and know that the contemplation of God and the word which is from Him suffice to nourish those who hear and stand to them in place of all food."[4] Some have explained the forty-day fasts of Moses, Elijah, and Jesus, not by appealing to supernatural sustenance but to the sheer enlivening power of the presence of God. They were, one might say, lifted from the realities and limitations of this world as they encountered the divine. Encountering God's utter holiness and deep love prompt fasting.

Basil the Great once wrote a letter to a monk who had fallen into adultery, in which he reminded that monk of the impact and ministry of his former rigorous fasting that was sustained by contemplating in the presence of God. "There I myself lived with you, and, for the toil of your ascetic discipline, called you blessed, *when fasting for weeks you continued in contemplation before God*, shunning the society of your fellows, like a routed runaway. . . . You emptied out all fats from your flesh; all the channels below your belly dried up. . . . You spent the long hours of the night in pouring out confession to God."[5] The very presence of God led this man to fast.

John Calvin knew the benefits of fasting to include better communion with God. Fasting, he wrote in *Institutes*, had three objectives—to subdue the flesh, to prepare for prayer and meditation, and to be a testimony of self-abasement before God. So, he recommends, "whenever men are to pray to God concerning any great matter, it would be expedient to appoint fasting along with prayer." Pointing to the example of the earliest

Christians, Calvin said their "sole purpose in this kind of fasting is to render themselves more eager and unencumbered for prayer,"[6] so they might commune with God more deeply.

A SUGGESTION

The Bible and the wisdom of the ages confirm that fasting and union with God are connected. What needs to be emphasized is that deepest traditions here reveal that fasting is a response to a sacred moment and not just an instrumental act we use to get what we want. If our desire is to deepen our love for God, to worship God more ravishingly, or to bask in God's grace, then that yearning for love and worship and grace can be permitted to do its natural work—that is, to lead us to fast. I believe God honors those who seek him this way, at times—not always—he may ravish our affections with his glorious presence.

10

FASTING AS
BODY HOPE

ONE THING THAT DISTINGUISHED EARLY CHRISTIANS from other groups who fasted was *body hope*—Christians fasted because they longed for Christ to return to establish the kingdom of God.[1] Flattened into a generic category, their fasting is personal embodiment of hope. In other words, sometimes we yearn so much for what we know God wants for this world, and sometimes we become so depressed over what our world is like in light of what God wants for us, that we are compelled to fast. Such fasting is body hope—we embody our hope by protesting the present conditions of this world.

JESUS AND BODY HOPE

Jesus taught his disciples to fast for the future. One time Jesus was approached with this comment: "John's disciples, like the disciples of the Pharisees, frequently fast and pray, but your disciples eat and drink" (Luke 5:33). Jesus was being asked to explain why his disciples were shucking tradition by not fasting. The word "frequently" (*pukna*) used in this verse could be translated as "intensely," referring both to the strength of Pharisees' commitment to fasting as well as its frequency. In concrete terms, both John's and the Pharisees' disciples are committed to fasting regularly. But Jesus' disciples are known instead for "eating and drinking"—that is, for *feasting* instead of fasting.

Obviously prepared for such a question, Jesus pushes back with a question for them: "You cannot make wedding guests fast while the bridegroom is with them, can you?" "Of course, you can't" is the answer. Which is precisely the point Jesus wants to establish: no one but a grouch fasts during a feast. But Jesus is not yet done.

"The days will come," Jesus predicts, "when the bridegroom will be taken away from them, and then they will fast in those days" (5:35). Two clever riddles are attached. As you don't sew a patch of new cloth on an old garment because the two won't match one another,[2] and as you don't put new wine in an old, thinned wineskin because the fermentation and expansion of gases will burst the old skin, so you don't fast when the bridegroom is present. But when the bridegroom is taken, you will fast.

JOHN AND JESUS ON FASTING

John the Baptist was well known for fasting. John's fasting was body hope for the kingdom of God. He couldn't get settled into this world until God's will was more firmly established. But Jesus saw things differently. What John was looking for, Jesus announced over and over, *is already here!* Jesus didn't fast for the future kingdom, because he believed that the future was present. Therefore, Jesus said, while he was in the world, fasting would be set aside.

Jesus develops his new perspective on the presence of that future with an image drawn from the prophets: the kingdom of God will be an endless messianic banquet of joy and fellowship and feasting. What is more, Jesus' own robust self-image enabled him to declare that eating with him at that time anticipated that very messianic banquet. Unlike John, who anticipated the kingdom and fasted for it, Jesus claimed the kingdom was present in him, and therefore it was time to end fasting and begin feasting.

But what happens when Jesus returns to the Father? During that time, Jesus predicts that his followers would resume fasting. Why? *To long for the day when God's messianic banquet and the just conditions of the kingdom would be established on earth as they are in heaven.* This kind of fast is nothing more than *embodying* the second and third petitions of the Lord's Prayer: "Your kingdom come/Your will be done, on earth as it is in heaven" (Matt. 6:10). One might even suggest that the fourth petition—"Give us this day our daily bread"—compares with God's sustaining of Moses, Elijah, and Jesus during their fasts. For Jesus, there are four periods, and fasting is special in each period: prior to Jesus, fasting for the Messiah; during the Messiah's time on earth, feasting; in anticipation of the coming fullness of the kingdom, fasting in hope; but once the kingdom has fully come, feasting will be the rule.

Pre-Jesus	Jesus' presence	Church	Kingdom
Fasting in anticipation	Feasting	Fasting in hope	Feasting

Fasting for the church, then, is a response to two sacred moments: the absence of Jesus and the recognition that this world is not what God intends it to be. Body hope responds to both of those by fasting.

WHAT ABOUT US?

Jesus predicted his followers would fast between his earthly incarnation and his final coming to renew the world, and they would fast during that time *as body hope that yearns for the kingdom.* Roman Catholic priest Thomas Ryan, whose book *The Sacred Art of Fasting* is one of the finest on the subject I have read, offers us some wise words:

Fasting is one of the ways the servants [of Jesus] keep themselves alert in this future-oriented waiting until the bridegroom returns. To what could you liken their discreet, mysterious joy as they wait? You could say it is like the quiet humming or whistling of a choir member earlier in the day of a concert. It's like a mother and father cleaning the house and making up the beds in anticipation of the kids' coming home at Thanksgiving or Christmas. It's like standing in the airport terminal or train station, waiting for your loved one to appear. It's like a fiancée patiently addressing the wedding invitations: The long-awaited event is not here yet, but it will come, and this is necessary preparation. In each case the energy is upbeat, forward-looking, and marked by the quiet joy of anticipation.[3]

Body hope as hoping for heaven is alive in the church. We find it among the Eastern Orthodox and among the Western Roman Catholic Church. But there is a need for a fresh revival of body hope that returns to the passage we have examined in this chapter and that focuses less on heaven and more on earth. Body hope is more like body poverty than body discipline, but its distinctive Christian character is that it is not just boycott against injustice but the embodiment of hope that God will act in this world to establish the divine will. To see how this body hope finds expression today, I want to focus on both the Eastern and Western church's statements and then turn to the significance of body hope for life on earth right now.

AN EASTERN PATH

The Eastern Orthodox fast as body hope, and they express this hope in the word *theosis*—that is, the hope of final, eternal, ecstatic union with God. "The aim" of the life of each and every Christian, the Orthodox teach, is "union [*henosis*] with God and deification [*theosis*]."[4] A colleague of mine, Bradley Nassif, is an Eastern Orthodox theologian. At the foundation of Eastern spirituality is the example of St. Anthony. My colleague wrote me this note, which I received at the very time I was editing this paragraph: "The 'sacred moment that prompts' Anthony's ascetic discipline is not so much a particular incident that served as a catalyst for fasting. Rather it was the 'eschatological vision' of the end of the age that shined a flashlight on the present moment. Because Christ is Risen, we fast, waiting for the coming return of the Bridegroom."[5] Eastern Christians, ideally, fast in order to align themselves more properly with God, and the formative process of fasting advances them in their journey into hope of union with God.

A WESTERN PATH

Everything about the Roman Catholic Church filters its way somehow through the *ecclesial life*, or the life of the church, and fasting as body hope fits into the Roman Catholic tradition admirably. Since God's redemptive work occurs in and through the grace of God manifest in the church (and its proper sacraments), fasting leads the Catholic Christian into participating in the church's life by creating solidarity with the poor and leading the body itself into the church's grace. Now, how does this fit with body hope? A genuine Roman Catholic theology of fasting is the embodied Christian orienting himself or herself toward the grace of God that *has* come, *is* coming, and *will* eventually come through and in the church, the bride of Christ, who will find herself outfitted in glory and honor in the final kingdom (Rev. 21–22). There is then a thread of body hope in all Catholic fasting: the Christian fasts in penitence, in order to give gifts to the poor, and in hope for the fullness of the body of Christ.

While I find the body hope themes in both the Eastern and Western churches of immense value for the church's life today, more can be said and more can be done if we want to recover what Jesus taught.

AN EARTHLY PATH

Christians can easily lose focus on their hope for God's kingdom. Sometimes our kingdom hope can be lost by focusing too much on a spiritual heaven or by concentrating too much on our personal needs. What Jesus taught his disciples to yearn for and to pray for was the manifestation of God's kingdom "on *earth* as it is in heaven" (Matt. 6:10, emphasis added). I believe body hope fasting is less focused on a heaven "up there," or even a heavenly personal spiritual union with God. Instead, body hope focuses more on God's love, peace, and justice being established here and now on earth. So when I read Jesus words about his followers fasting before he returns, I hear Jesus summoning his followers to long for and hope for God's perfect kingdom to be realized *on earth.*

Body hope embodies the Christian yearning for moral, social, and political improvement in his world, for evangelism, for families living in love and for communities striving for the common good—in short, for manifestations of the kingdom of God in the now. Kent Berghuis, whose study and practice of fasting has challenged my own understanding at numerous points, puts it best when he says that "the Christian era is an age of fasting and feasting, of holding the tension of unfinished business, while confessing in faith to the outcome."[6]

> Christ has come—we can feast.
> Christ is yet to come—we should fast.

During the Church Age, as we glance back a few pages at the chart, we both feast (because Christ is with us) and fast (as we anticipate the kingdom) because we yearn for God to establish the kingdom of God on earth.

PART 2

WISDOM AND FASTING

11

FASTING AND
ITS PROBLEMS

AS SOON AS FASTING CLIMBED TO THE TOP OF THE CHART OF
signs of piety, its problems began to appear. The first recorded
assault on fasting was that of Isaiah 58, wherein the prophet,
whose accusations were straight from the moouth of the Lord (v.
14), pointed long fingers and fixed his sharp eyes on those who
thought they were the fasting pious but who were also the unlov-
ing and unjust. Ever since Isaiah, Jews, Christians, and Muslims
have warned others about the hypocrisies that find their way into
fasting, and all have pointed to the importance of an inner life that
transcends the physical act of fasting. Sometimes the criticisms
root themselves so deeply into a person's or church's conscience
that fasting collapses into the valley of bygone spiritual disciplines.

Suggest to your friends that you are into body discipline,
and chances are you will hear a litany of problems with fasting.
Here are some of the most common problems, and I briefly
discuss these in no particular order, but each is important.
Knowing the potential problems with a spiritual discipline can
help us practice that discipline more faithfully.

MANIPULATION

When my children were very young and answered a question from their mom or me, sometimes we'd ask them a follow-up question: "Do you really mean what you are saying?" They would inevitably say, "I really mean it." When they were especially emphatic, they'd say, "I really, really, really mean it." This reveals that sometimes what we say we do not mean, so we have to prop up our simple claims with words assuring others we are telling the truth. As "I really, really, really mean it" implies that "I mean it" might not be squarely true, so fasting can become our "I really mean it" with God. Some Christians think fasting proves to God their utter seriousness and deep devotion. *God, so they think, will be especially attentive to my prayer if I fast.* Nonsense. God cannot be manipulated or badgered into giving us what we want. This view of fasting, which is an extreme instrumental view, too easily slides into manipulation.

Sometimes manipulation comes from other Christians and works in the other direction. Instead of the Christian trying to manipulate God, some Christians manipulate others by demanding fasting as an inevitable sign of piety and using it to judge the lesser piety of those who don't fast. But fasting is not the special mark of piety. The singular marks of piety in the New Testament are these: loving God, loving others, and living in the Spirit. Since these are hard to judge in others, we are sometimes tempted to "mark" piety by spiritual disciplines such as fasting. This is a mistake, and it can lead to suffering and depression on the part of Christians who struggle with fasting but who genuinely love God, love others, and walk in the Spirit.

CHEATING AND LEGALISM

Most of us know that fasting can be a challenge, and it is even more of a challenge when we are fasting with others. The stakes are raised the more seriously the group believes the fast is vital for the concern. Some fasters fail to achieve their own personal goal or that of the group. For whatever reasons—hunger pains are the major issue—they may nibble on something or eat just a little bit. They have both broken the fast and their own word—not to mention their commitment to the group. This is a common problem in fasting, and the earliest writers on the subject all know it and urge Christians to stick to their word.

At this point, unfortunately, some fear they have committed the sin of Achan (found in Joshua 7), who swiped some things that had been devoted to destruction. Israel's next battle against Ai led to a defeat, and it was revealed to Israel that someone had contaminated the sacred community by cheating. Achan had stolen a Babylonian robe, two hundred shekels of silver, and a bar of gold, and he had hidden them under his tent. Achan was found out, and he was stoned. Today, some with supersensitive consciences feel they might get "stoned" by the group if they confess that they have not kept the fast properly. So they lie and tell others they fasted. Here is where we all need to be honest and open: any community that practices fasting needs also to talk about the difficulties we all face with hunger pains and that on some days we simply don't endure. Any community that doesn't tolerate normal struggles with fasting or permit flexibility will damage its own witness, and the spiritual freedom of its members will be constricted by legalism.

Not every fast turns out well; sometimes we forget and eat something accidentally. Sometimes we can't resist the urge to eat. When we break our fast before its appointed time, we have simply failed to keep what we have committed ourselves to. When this happens, we should not take our failure lightly, but neither should we see it as an unforgivable sin. In such cases, confess your laxity, carelessness, or weakness of will to the God of all mercy, tell your group what happened, and resolve to do better next time. And I counsel groups to be merciful to your fellow fasters—fasting is not easy for all.

PETTY CASUISTRY

To fast means to deny oneself of food and possibly also water in response to a sacred moment. Casuistry is the multiplication of rules to prevent one from breaking a more significant law. Petty casuistry is getting around the law (fasting) by defining it too narrowly. Here's how it can happen with fasting. Fasting, so the "law" would be, is about denying oneself of *food*, but since (so it is argued in petty casuistry) fasting is really concerned with "pleasure," one need only deny oneself of pleasurable foods. Thus, one is fasting if one is denying oneself of red meats or desserts, but it is okay to eat lima beans (Lord, have mercy).

No one exposed petty casuistry with more rhetorical flourish than Martin Luther when he wrote about those who considered denial of a particular kind of food (meat) or drink (wine) an opportunity to eat or drink more of something else. That's not fasting, Luther told them all:

> For I really dare say that in what they termed "fasting" in the papacy I never saw a genuine fast. How can I call it a fast if someone prepares a lunch of expensive fish, with the choicest spices, more and better than for two or three other meals, and washes it down with the strongest drink, and spend an hour or three at filling his belly till it is stuffed? Yet that was the usual thing and a minor thing even among the very strictest monks. But it was the holy fathers, the bishops, the abbots, and the other prelates who were really strict in their observance, with ten and twenty courses and so much refreshment at night that several threshers could have lived on it for three days.[1]

He's right when he concludes this: "It irks me that some people should practice and permit this mockery in Christendom, deceiving God with the mask of saying that such a life of gluttony and guzzling and belly-filling should be called a fast and a good work."[2] This is petty casuistry of the worst sort.

I do not doubt that some did fast in order to feast. Nor do I doubt that Luther's words are both exaggerated and bombastic—plenty of Roman Catholic leaders of his day fasted, as is fitting for a Christian. Nor do I doubt that Luther's words would have led many to conclude that "if this is what fasting is, we shouldn't fast at all." We should take his words as an exaggerated lesson of what our petty casuistries can sometimes do to us.

HYPOCRISY

From Isaiah to Jesus to Justin Martyr's *Dialogue with Trypho* to the early Christian *Epistle of Barnabas* to Martin Luther to every book you can find on fasting at your local bookstore, the story is the same: Christian, beware of hypocrisy if you choose to fast! I like how Basil said it when warning of the dangers of not being transformed morally while fasting: "This safe where you keep your valuables isn't secure; there are holes in the bottom of your wine-bottles. The wine at least leaks out, and runs down its own path; but sin remains inside."[3] If your fast doesn't lead you to deeper love for God and others or to a more complete holiness, your spirituality is leaky!

Jerome, a fourth-century church father with a rigorous disposition, who supervised a monastery in Bethlehem, said this well in a lengthy letter to a certain Eustochium: "If you have fasted two or three days, do not think yourself better than others who do not fast. You fast and are angry; another eats and wears a smiling face. You work off your irritation and hunger in quarrels. He uses food in moderation and gives God thanks."[4] The point: being good is the goal of fasting. If you are not discovering some moral improvement, you are not fasting aright. By all means, he was saying, let us not be hoodwinked into thinking that fasting is the point of spirituality.

Saint John Chrysostom, in his famous early Christian homilies on the gospel of Matthew, said, "For of what use is fasting when the mind is full of wickedness; when you blame others, when you condemn them [while] bearing about beams in your eyes and do all for display?"[5] And I love this homiletical gem from Chrysostom: "Though you should fast, though you should lie upon the ground and even strangle yourself, but take no thought for your neighbor, you have worked nothing great but still stand far from this Image [Christ] while so doing."[6]

If our fasting does not lead to growth in love and holiness, fasting can become hypocritical. Fasting is a response to a grievous sacred moment, and contact with the sacred ought to transform us. The rule to follow is a simple one: fasting, like all the spiritual disciplines, is designed to develop love of God and love of others. If it is not doing that, something is wrong.

ATTENTION

Alongside hypocrisy, some Christians use fasting to get attention. They fast because of the glory it brings them. The logic is obvious:

Everyone thinks Christians who fast are pious.
I fast.
Therefore, others will think I'm pious.

As Jesus put it: "They have received their reward" (Matt. 6:16). In other words, attention is all they will get. Jesus' strategy was as good then as it is now: when we fast, we should tell no one who does not need to know, and we need not smear ashes on our faces to make it obvious what we are doing. If the mark of ashes for you is a mark of distinction, wash it off.

These are not rules—the warning Jesus gave was for those who wore fasting as badge for attention. Some could fast in sackcloth and with ashes or with dust scattered on their heads, and they did with utter focus. Others need to be warned to erase any traces of piety.[7]

MERITORIOUSNESS

If the graphic critique by Martin Luther had any merit, the charge of meritoriousness has had even greater play. Namely, that in fasting many are seeking the favor of God and thinking that fasting is meritorious in God's eyes. Because this was such a common protest by Luther and his successors, and because it has also been a favorite card played by critics of Catholicism, I will raise the issue of merit in that context—but I will be the first to declare that meritoriousness is no more a sin of Catholics than any other Christian denomination. The problem here is not Catholicism; the problem is humans who think they can gain favor before God by what they do.

The singular Protestant impulses are *sola gratia* and *sola fide*—by (God's) grace alone and by faith alone. That is, one cannot do anything to merit God's favor; God showers his grace upon us because of his mercy and love, not because we have earned it. Luther said, "Fasting has become a means of seeking great merit before God, of atoning for sin, and of reconciling God."[8] This problem of converting fasting from spontaneous and natural body talk in response to a grievous sacred moment into merit occurred prior to the life of Jesus and sometime after the Hebrew Bible (the Old Testament). So the noncanonical Psalms of Solomon says, "The righteous constantly searches his house, to remove his unintentional sins. He atones for sins of ignorance by fasting and humbling his soul" (Pss. Sol. 3:7–8).

This problem remains with us today: if we fast and then think we've done something God should not only take special note of but for which he should also give us special blessings because we've gone the extra mile, then we are mistaken regarding what fasting is all about.

BENEFIT-ITIS

I'm not in the habit of neologisms, but I think this idea of *benefit-itis* works. Some folks spend so much time thinking of what they can get from fasting that they see the entire scope of the discipline of fasting through the lens of what it does for us. Again, the instrumental view of fasting gains the upper hand. Today, we are often not one or two pages into an exhortation for Christians to begin fasting before the exhorter is convincing us that if we fast we'll be more spiritual, more attentive to God, more focused spiritually, more often the receptor of God's gifts, more healthy, more . . . more . . . more. The inflammation of things we will get from fasting is what I call benefit-itis.

Again, this is nonsense. Fasting in the deep traditions of the Bible is not about what we get but about our response to life's sacred moments. We fast because the moment we face is so sacred that fasting is the only way for us to bring our entire person before God. We don't fast to get something from God; we fast to express ourselves to God most completely. Sometimes, to be sure, our intent is to gain something we seek from God (see chapter 4 on body plea), but we don't think fasting is the way we'll get that benefit. Instead, we are so serious about our plea that we have to fast to express it properly—and we plead with God for something by fasting.

Let me say this a little differently: fasting is not even about clearing a space for God; it is not about being more open to God. Fasting is how we find expression when we, before God, are wholly intent on God as we encounter one of life's sacred moments. To focus on what we get from fasting misconstrues the glory of the human experience.

HEALTH

Some contend that fasting is good for the body. Psychologists warn that fasting can lead to anorexia nervosa—which it can. Your local physician might warn you that fasting can mess up your electrolytes if you overdo it. So any contention that fasting will make you healthier must be the advice of your medical doctor. And, because this subject is so important, the last chapter of this book will be about the medical dimensions of fasting.

EXTREMISM

Some of us know or have read or heard about people who began with a weekly fast but were soon led into more and more rigorous forms of fasting where they were flagellating themselves and wearing haircloth or sackcloth and were so emaciated one had to wonder about their sanity. This is the danger of extremism. Fasting, like everything else, must be done properly and in the right balance.

I think here of Jerome's revealing comments about his extremist ascetic and fasting lifestyle:

Tears and groans were every day my portion; and if drowsiness chanced to overcome my struggles against it, my bare bones, which hardly held together, clashed against the ground. Of my food and drink I say nothing: for, even in sickness, the solitaries have nothing but cold water, and to eat one's food cooked is looked upon as self-indulgence. Now, although in my fear of hell I had consigned myself to this prison [in the desert], where I had no companions but scorpions and wild beats, I often found myself amid bevies of [fantasized] girls. My face was pale and my frame chilled with fasting; yet my mind was burning with desire, and the fires of lust kept bubbling up before me when my flesh was as good as dead.

But, he also adds that "I sometimes felt myself among angelic hosts."[9]

John Cassian warns of the danger of extremes and what his life was like when he was a radical ascetic:

For I remember that I had so often resisted the desire for food,
that having abstained from taking any food for two or three
days, my mind was not troubled even by the recollection of
any eatables and also that sleep was by the assaults of the devil
so far removed from my eyes that for several days and nights
I used to pray the Lord to grant a little sleep to my eyes; and
then I felt I was in greater peril from the want [lack] of food
and sleep than from struggling against sloth and gluttony.

He concludes with this after long years of experience:
"excessive abstinence is still more injurious to us than careless
satiety."[10] Or as Jerome put it so cleverly when saying we all need
our breaks from fasting and that everyone needs to eat: "I have
learned by experience that the ass toiling along the highway
makes for an inn when it is weary."[11]

There is no reason here to suggest that all fasting is bad
because fasting can lead to extremism. But neither is there any
reason to avoid the warning that fasting can lead, in the hands
of the most rigorous, to extremes that are healthy neither for
the body nor the soul—not to mention the church itself. This
book does not devote its attention to asceticism, but it is not
hard to see that rigorous fasting and the ascetic lifestyle often
walk hand in hand, and sometimes to the detriment of the person's spirituality. Jerome knew of radicals who as a result of too
much fasting "[did]not know what to do or where to turn,
when to speak and when to be silent."[12]

FAT TUESDAY

On Fat Tuesday, the tradition is for revelers to fatten up, eat all the meat they can and drink all they can, because Lent begins on Ash Wednesday. It's a stereotype to be sure.

But the tradition is older than what happens in New Orleans these days. John Chrysostom poked his finger at this issue in the fourth century and aimed his barbs at the men of his churches:

> But since many men, both when about to enter upon the fast, as if the belly were on the point of being delivered over to a sort of lengthened siege, lay in beforehand a stock of gluttony and drunkenness; and again, on being set at liberty [at the end of the Lenten fast], going forth as from a long famine and grievous prison, run to the table with unseemly greediness, just as if they were striving to undo again the advantage gained through the fast, by an excess of gluttony."[13]

Indulging before or after a fast is not the point of fasting— nor is it healthy.

Having warned ourselves of the dangers of fasting, it is now time to turn to the age-old question: are there any benefits in fasting?

12

FASTING AND
ITS BENEFITS

HAVING ALREADY LAID MY CARDS ON THE TABLE FOR
what I think of fasting for the benefits one gets, we still have to
examine what benefits there are for those who fast. John Piper,
a pastor in Minnesota, tells the story of Carl Lundquist, a college president for three decades who learned to fast in his later
years. After Lundquist witnessed the impact of fasting in Korea
as told to him by Dr. Joon Gon Kim, who had fasted for forty
days in response to a grievous situation and yearned to turn
back a political decision, Lundquist makes this statement: "As I
went back to the hotel I reflected that I had never fasted like
that." Here's the point we are illustrating: Lundquist says,
"Perhaps I had never desired a work of God with the same
intensity."[1] My contention is that it is the desire, the yearning,
the "want-it-ness" that gives rise to the kind of fasting that benefits the one fasting. Fasting is the natural response of a person

who, to put it bluntly, "wants it" and wants what she or he wants in response to a situation that is grievous.

A WARNING

The first thing to say must be said abruptly: *there may be no immediate and noticeable benefits in fasting.* David fasted before God for the life of his son, and the son died. Millions of Christians have fasted for millions of reasons and their pleas were not answered as they wanted them to be answered. Some people fast to conquer a sin and find no victory. Some fast in order to connect more intimately with God and find only a thick wall between them and God. So this must be put on the table before anything else is said: fasting is not magical, and there are no guarantees. Fasting is not a technique we ply that makes things happen just because we ply it. To return to our columns, the heart of the deep Christian tradition about fasting is that a grievous sacred moment (A) prompts the integrated person to fast (B). Sometimes the resolution (C) comes about, and sometimes it doesn't.

Fasting is what happens to the person who yields the whole person—body, soul, spirit, heart, and mind—to God. And like the Pevensie children in the Chronicles of Narnia who sometimes found the wardrobe a passage into Narnia and other times nothing but a wooden enclosure leading to nowhere, so also the surrender to God: sometimes the fasting person is ushered into Narnia and sometimes not. Opening the wardrobe door, just like fasting, is no guarantee the back of the wardrobe will merge into Narnia.

But this leads me back to the line of argument in this book: fasting is body talk. We fast, not because by fasting we will gain a closer hearing from God but because it is the best and most integrated response to life's sacred moments. There is a joy in simply communicating wholly with God. Communication with God is, in my opinion, the intent of fasting.

Still, too many Christians through the ages have had much come to them after they have fasted for us to ignore the benefits of fasting—as long as (to repeat a point) we don't think it is the fasting that brings the benefit. All good gifts come from God; we lay ourselves before God and sometimes we get what we want and sometimes we don't. But the prayer of a righteous person is heard, James informs us (5:16)—and sometimes the righteous find that fasting is the only way to express themselves. So, in what follows we discover that the person who yields herself or himself completely to God sometimes discovers space for God, freedom from sin, answers to prayer, and justice for the poor. Perhaps I can begin with one of the most significant treatises ever written on prayer, Basil's sermon "About Fasting":

Fasting gives birth to prophets, she strengthens the powerful.
Fasting makes lawmakers wise.

She is a safeguard of a soul, a stabilizing companion to the
body, a weapon for the brave, a discipline for champions.
Fasting knocks over temptations, anoints for godliness.
She is a companion for sobriety, the crafter of a sound mind.
In wars she fights bravely, in peace she teaches tranquility.
She sanctifies the Nazirite, and she perfects the priest.[2]

SPACE FOR GOD

A person who is totally open to God and responds to life's
sacred moments with fasting can discover the life-giving presence of God and sometimes a palpable experience of God's
presence. Adam and Eve, the archetype story of the Bible, lived
in God's presence in Eden but were banished from Eden.
Humans, the Bible is telling us, were designed to enjoy intimacy
with God but are alienated by their own will. Yet, deep within
the heart of each human is a cup that knows and yearns for its
desired drink. Or, as St. Augustine put it, "You have made us
for yourself, and our heart is restless till it finds its rest in you."[3]
Just as important, St. Augustine provokes that thought with this
statement: "You stir us up to take delight in your praise."[4]
Humans, the entire Christian tradition informs us, yearn for
God, and it is God at work in each to create that yearning. For
some that divinely implanted yearning, surely one of life's
sacred moments, for the palpable presence of God is so intense

that they fast. One might say that the hidden presence of God is so intense for some that they fast in order to break through into the palpable presence of God. However one describes this, there are those who seek for God, whose seeking finds expression in fasting, and who find that presence.

Moses' own yearning for God might express just this point (Ex. 34). Was it Moses' fast that led to his face-to-face experience with God, or was it the presence of God that created an environment where eating would destroy the sanctity of the moment? Fasting expresses the yearning of an entire presence to know the presence of God, and that yearning creates space for God just as the presence of God creates a yearning so intense for God's presence that fasting results.

The same can be said for Jesus (Matt. 4:1–11). At the outset of his public ministry, with thirty years of prayer and praxis behind him and a public identification with John the Baptist's vision for God's redemptive plan just completed, Jesus is driven by God's Spirit into a desert where he communes with his Father. It is no wonder that Jesus fasted for forty days and nights. In the barren wilderness, Jesus relives Israel's forty years of wandering—only this time, unlike the children of Israel, Jesus remains obedient because he sanctifies himself in fasting before the very presence of God. Not even the devil's suggestion that Jesus use his powers to redo the manna miracle will deter Jesus from the sacredness of that time with God.

John Wesley knew this from experience: "Then [in prayer

and fasting] especially it is that God is often pleased to lift up the souls of his servants above all the things of earth, and sometimes to rap them up, as it were, into the third heaven."[5]

The singular emphasis on this today is given by John Piper, who has brought his personal vision of passion for God's glory to bear on nearly every subject pertaining to the Christian life. In Piper's book on fasting, called *A Hunger for God*, Piper explains fasting as the soul's yearning for intimacy with God and that fasting reminds us of our soul's greatest yearning—to take pleasure in God's pleasure. He puts it all together with this statement: "Half of Christian fasting is that our physical appetite is lost because our homesickness for God is so intense. The other half is that our homesickness for God is threatened because our physical appetites are so intense."[6]

FREEDOM FROM BAD HABITS

Perhaps owing to the focus on fasting in Dallas Willard's influential book *The Spirit of the Disciplines*, with its emphasis on Christians learning to train themselves by disciplining themselves,[7] the major incentive of fasting in the Christian tradition today seems to focus on the benefit of gaining freedom from bad habits. If the apostle Paul speaks of beating his own body into subjection (1 Cor. 9:27), it should not surprise us that many Christians have followed his steps. "More than any other

Discipline," Richard Foster claims, "fasting reveals the things that control us." A simple fast of a few hours will get the stomach churning and the faster will be challenged to continue the fast by fighting through the desire to eat, or the person will learn to say no to the desire. If the desire overcomes, the person learns something about herself or himself. But, as Foster goes on to say, fasting reveals more than the hunger for food: "If pride controls us, it will be revealed almost immediately." He continues: "Anger, bitterness, jealousy, strife, fear—if they are within us, they will surface during fasting."[8]

We are not sure today why Jesus' contemporaries fasted on Mondays and Thursdays—perhaps to discipline themselves morally and maybe as body hope. We are reasonably confident that a major motivation for the early Christian stationary fast on Wednesdays and Fridays was body discipline in order to gain in their conformity to Christ. If that kind of fasting revealed to the person what most controlled them, those folks knew what to work on next. If disciplinary fasting taught the subordination of desire to spirit, bad habits had a chance of being reduced. If the Christian joined those days of fasting to face God with a particular bad habit or sinful practice, that person could make progress.

Nearly everyone who fasts realizes in one way or another that fasting makes us deeply aware that food sustains us, and this realization leads us to be grateful to God for our food. Gratitude leads one to perceive that we are dependent upon

God, and when we can achieve this realization we can make genuine moral progress in life.

ANSWERS TO PRAYER

In the Old Testament, Ezra advised those returning to the promised land to fast and pray for God's guidance and protection, and they received it. Saul's companions sought God's mind with fasting and were given guidance. The basic intuition of humans to seek the mind of God remains to this day. Many fast as they seek to know what they think God wants them to do. Students wondering which major to choose, parents worrying about their children's futures, adults concerned about making ends meet, lovers fighting their way through relational wrinkles—each of these has found that fasting can help in discovering the next step, the right step, or the wise step to take.

JUSTICE FOR THE POOR

Isaiah 58 finds its way into every element of fasting: the genuine fast is to get beyond ourselves to do good for the other. Genuine fasting leads to seeking justice. Fasting reveals our need for food, and that revelation can make us more aware of the needs of others that in turn can prompt us not only to give them what we would have spent (or eaten), but to flow into a life of generosity and involvement and fighting for justice for the poor and needy in our world.

Recently a friend told me that during Lent she ate only what the rest of the world's poor ate: grains. So during the entire Lent, she was focused on the condition of the poor—and if that doesn't make us more charitable, few things will.

A REMINDER

Now a reminder: I do believe that there are tangible, real, beneficial results from fasting, but I also believe that fasting is not an instrument that can be utilized to get what we want. Instead, we need to put each of these benefits of fasting into the larger context of fasting: each of these benefits emerges out of a response to some kind of sacred moment. In response to these sacred moments—disaster, death, desires—we turn to face God. It is in that turning, as we turn to God in faith and in hope and in love, that God can bring about the results that undo the grievous situation we faced. This, I think, is the proper way to see fasting in the Christian tradition.

13

FASTING AND
THE BODY

ONCE A CLEVER PASTOR, INTENT ON DRAWING A LAUGH at my expense and perhaps a bit suspicious of too much schooling on my part, introduced me as having "the kind of doctorate that doesn't do anybody any good." Even if I question what he means by "any good"—after all, we theologians do study about and try to live the "good"—I don't question that what he said applies to the subject I now turn to in this chapter. I am not a medical doctor, and in what follows I am relying totally on experts who have come my way.[1] What happens to the body when we stop eating? Or when we engage in fasting? Is it healthy to fast?

FASTING AND THE ANCIENT WORLD

Let's be clear about this to begin with: fasting in the Bible does not emerge from health concerns, it is neither dieting nor cleansing, and a grade schooler today perceives the working of the body more accurately than ancient Israelites and early Christians.[2] We must be exceedingly cautious about drawing medical conclusions about health from the pages of the Bible or early Christian theorizing about the body. We must also be careful of suggesting that an ancient spiritual discipline such as fasting was done to support our theories about health and diet.

Some early Christians were persuaded that a light and dry diet was good for the soul while heavy and moist foods and drinks led to evil thoughts. Most of this goes back in one way or another to Galen, a second-century Greek doctor/philosopher from Asia Minor. There are, he argued, four elements (fire, earth, air, and water), four qualities (warm, cold, dry, and moist), and four body fluids or humors (blood, black bile, yellow bile, phlegm).

Good health, Galen mistakenly believed, emerges from the proper mixture (Greek *krasis*) of each of these elements. The four body fluids result from the sorts of foods one eats. Soul health follows from body health, which means that the proper mixture of fluids generated by sound diet. As an example, wine heats and moistens the body while barley cools the body. Warmer foods produce bile, while cooler foods produce phlegm. The sexual energies of a human being were like the steam in an espresso machine—love brought one's blood to a boil and converted the blood into the "crema" of semen. Fasting, or even changing diet to drier foods, could cool the sexual desires and lead to a more chaste life. Dieting and moral health then interact with one another. (Medically, of course, if one does not sufficiently eat, one's passions, including sexual desires, will diminish.)

We could go on, but the point is clear: the ancients were doing their best to explain the workings of the human body, but they were a long way from scientific accuracy about the body and therefore with their correlations of bodily health with moral health.

FASTING'S DANGER

Let's also be clear about this: fasting, if not done intelligently and in line with sound health principles, can damage the body. John Wesley wrote to Richard Morgan, whose son had been in the original circle of Oxford Methodists, with these words: "On Sunday last I was informed (as no doubt you will be e'er long) that my brother and I had killed your son; that the rigorous fasting which he had imposed upon himself, by our advice, had increased his illness and hastened his death." Wesley defended himself.[3] The story remains a warning to anyone who chooses to fast in a rigorous fashion without sound advice from a medical professional—fasting deprives the body of what it needs and must be done with care and intelligence. Let's be honest here: fasting of more than a few hours—in its most graphic term—starves the body.

A brutal condition of excessive dieting today is anorexia nervosa, and the wise leaders of churches will especially warn our youth of the dangers of fasting because of these kinds of conditions. Alongside parents, pastors and leaders need to monitor the fasting of teenagers. Some youth will fast for no other reason than to be thin, and if not guarded with the utmost of care, such behavior can lead to anorexia. A friend of mine recently said to me that he would never encourage a group of young adults to fast because of its potential harmful implications.

FASTING AND MODERN MEDICINE

In disagreement with what some health specialists routinely claim about the invigoration of health through fasting or cleansing, many medical doctors counter with this: fasting doesn't "cleanse" the colon or give a rest to other organs but instead disturbs the electrolyte balance, eliminates some of the necessary good bacteria, and makes the blood more acidic. Fasting leads to the body feeding on itself—on muscle and protein. Fasting, doctors may inform you, does not cleanse the body but instead increases metabolic toxins and decreases blood pressure. However, fasting does not harm the body if proper hydration occurs and as long as the fast does not endure more than a dozen or so hours.

Much of health-directed "fasting" is really about health

and weight loss or about the pleasant feelings generated by a lighter body. Medical doctors care for the body and know that being overweight is unhealthy, so a proper diet that reduces the body weight to an ideal leads both to health and a longer life. But the proper method for getting to one's ideal weight is neither radical fasting nor the religious excuse of fasting, but a sound diet, the appropriate consumption of calories, and proper exercise.

My warning is this: fasting in the Bible is not about dieting and is not shaped by health concerns. Fasting, if not done properly, can potentially damage the body. Two medical doctors recently said to me that they can think of nothing good for the body that can come through fasting. (Both stated that weight loss for the overweight is a good thing, but fasting wasn't the appropriate method for weight loss.)

I'm not a medical doctor and am relying on these doctors' professional results. I realize that many health experts and fasting proponents are unafraid to declare the benefits to our health from fasting, but I stand with the medical team on this matter: fasting is potentially damaging to the body. I urge you to fast only under clear and safe conditions. And if you have any doubts, you need to check with your family physician. Work your way into the discipline of fasting by fasting from breakfast to dinner and then perhaps skipping breakfast and having lunch and then, if one finds the body capable of sustaining that kind of fast, fasting from one dinner to the next.

Fasting should not be done by diabetics, children, women who are pregnant or nursing, and by those with serious diseases, who are sick, or who are infirm.

FASTING: WHAT HAPPENS?

Take a fresh piece of salmon. Before you put the salmon on a skillet, turn the heat to high and get the pan red-hot. Now put the salmon on the skillet; you will sear the salmon. Walk away for fifteen minutes or so, and then return to your smoking skillet and burned salmon. (I'm not really recommending you do this unless you are outside!) Before I make my point, let me suggest an alternative. Take a fresh piece of salmon, gently drizzle both sides with some extra-virgin olive oil—perhaps with some porcini mushroom flavoring to it—and let it sit in a refrigerator for an hour or so. Then heat the skillet to medium or just a tad higher, gently place the salmon on the skillet for four to six minutes, and then turn the salmon steak over and grill on the other side for four to six minutes.

To use this analogy, some people fast so rigorously the body burns up all of its stored energies and they jeopardize their health—Catherine of Siena and St. Francis are two good examples. Other people drizzle a gentle diet of fasting throughout their lives—sometimes spontaneously and sometimes with a disciplinary rhythm, but never to an extreme. Such people find fasting to be a good spiritual discipline. Which is the wiser way? The answer is obvious.

If you don't know what you are doing to your body when you fast, you increase your chance of "burning out" much sooner. What more of us need is a scientific awareness of what fasting does to us medically. So what happens to the body when we fast?

THE BASICS

Staying with our salmon analogy, the body needs "oil" to survive the heat of life. That is, the body needs energy—in the form of glucose that results mostly from carbohydrates that are broken into glucose through digestive enzymes. We eat the salmon, and the body converts salmon into energy. The body needs these "oils" to keep cells happy and healthy and to create metabolism and energy and everything else all our insides were created to do. We eat, and the body machine keeps on clicking, and our cells sing their own kind of song and do their own kind of dancing.

But when we stop eating in order to fast, we put ourselves onto the hot skillet of life with no oils—the carbohydrates are not available for glucose production, so the body adjusts to keep itself alive. The body knows what to do—it seeks energy by heading straight to the "emergency food cellars"—that is, to the liver and muscles, where there are some little packets of stored resources to use for emergencies. The liver's little food cellar also holds several pounds of water, so fasting leads to the depletion of this water, and that means some rather rapid weight loss as the body spends the food resources in the liver.

POTENTIAL HARM

Potential harmful symptoms of excessive fasting include iron deficiency, rapid B vitamin depletion, as well as dilution of fat and muscle mass. This leads to all kinds of symptoms if fasting continues, including a body condition called *ketosis*. When we stop eating, the body finds something in the body that can be converted into energy. When the carbohydrates disappear, the body turns to fats. Ketosis is the abnormal accumulation of ketones—a by-product of metabolizing fatty acids—caused by the inefficient supply of carbohydrates. When the normal provision of glucose is interrupted by an insufficient supply of carbohydrates, the body turns to fats and milks the fats for energy supplies. Conversion of fats into energy releases fatty acids into the blood, where they are converted into ketones. Medical professionals do not see ketosis as a favorable condition for health. Among other things, the acid buildup in the blood can predispose the person to serious if not fatal heart rhythm disturbances.

In the *Cecil Textbook of Medicine*, we read of how quickly the body begins to invade the body's emergency resources:

By 24 hours of fasting, the use of glucose [our body's natural and preferred source of energy] as a fuel has decreased;

only 15% of liver glycogen stores remain. . . . After 3 days of fasting, the rate of glucose production is reduced by one half and the rate of lipolysis is more than double the values found at 12 hours of fasting. . . . By 7 days of fasting, plasma ketone body concentrations have increased 75-fold and ketone bodies provide 70% of the brain's energy needs.[4]

We have probably given enough (or more than enough) information for our purposes—the body adjusts to fasting, but only to keep itself alive.

We are not created to live in the emergency rooms of our bodies. Fasting, in other words, threatens the stability of the body's health.

KETOSIS: GOOD OR BAD?

As the body empties the resources in the liver and muscles through ketosis, there is a constant discharge of acidic toxins into the body that can only be called poisoning the body. (By the way, ketosis generates the unpleasantries of bad breath and smelly skin!) When the body begins to use ketones for its "oil," the body is degenerating (or hibernating or cooking itself) because the body recognizes ketosis as the onset of starvation. Many fasters and some health specialists see value in ketosis, and some even describe heightened spiritual sensitivity and a contentment in a lack of appetite (which is not healthy) during ketosis. Medical professionals, however, recognize ketosis as a form of starvation and know that its radical form, ketoacidosis, is a dangerous condition for the human body.

The body can maintain itself on ketosis for about forty days and during this time most experience a lack of appetite—among other things, none of them healthy. About forty days into a rigorous fast of water alone (some drink juice as well), the body again develops an appetite (because it knows if it doesn't get food, it will starve and die). If one prolongs a fast beyond this, serious damage can be done to the body.

Furthermore, after the body uses up a significant amount of its fat reserves for fuel, it begins to break down protein. This will result in muscle weakness that can take months to rebuild.

CONCLUSION

I close this chapter on this note: fasting is what happens to the unified person who encounters a moment so sacred—a death, a consciousness of sin, a need to stand before God in prayer, a desire for holiness and love—that the person simply can't eat—the moment is too sacred to indulge in food or pleasure. Our bodies need foods and fuels to survive; it is our responsibility to recognize this. We are to live before God, ourselves, and others in a way that knows the difference between the sacredness of eating and the sacredness of fasting.

CONCLUSION

WE BEGAN THIS BOOK WITH A DEFINITION OF FASTING, and as we close, I want to bring this definition to your attention one more time:

Fasting is the natural, inevitable response of a person to a grievous sacred moment in life.

The elements of this definition should now be clear. Fasting is the choice not to eat or drink for a specified period. Fasting is not the same as abstinence, which is the choice not to eat or drink specific items even though one is still eating and drinking other items. Neither is fasting the same as dieting, which is the choice not to eat or drink various items for health reasons. Fasting, as we see it in the biblical tradition, emerges from an organic and unified sense of the whole person—body and spirit (or soul) acting in consort. For the unified person, fasting is both *natural* and *inevitable* when that person encounters sacred moments in life.

Now we come to the heart of the biblical traditions about fasting: fasting is a *response*. When particular kinds of events in life occur, fasting is the way the unified person naturally and inevitably responds. We have emphasized that responsive fasting deserves more attention today and that the more commonly practiced form of fasting deserves less attention. What is the more common form? We call it *instrumental* fasting. Instrumental fasting is the choice to fast in order to get something or gain something from the fast. We can now remind ourselves of the three elements of fasting, the A ➔ B ➔ C flow in fasting.

A	B	C
Sacred Moment	**Fasting**	**Results**

In this book, our emphasis has been on B as a response to A. This is where the depth of the Christian tradition is found. The more recent emphasis of fasting in order to get, the B leading to C, however important, is not the biblical emphasis.

What makes all of this come together is to understand that fasting is a response to a *grievous sacred moment*. Fasting is a natural and inevitable response to the following:

- sin
- death
- impending disaster or disaster itself
- the lack of holiness and love and compassion
- the impoverishment of others
- the sacred presence of God
- the absence of justice, peace, and love

Fasting is the whole person responding to each of these, so we have called these kinds of responses *body turning, body grief body plea, body discipline, body poverty,* and *body contact* (with God), and *body hope.* A particularly notable feature of many religious traditions, beginning with the Hebrew Bible and flowing into the earliest Christian movement, and then centuries later into Islam, is to set aside specific dates in the year to remember sacred moments like these and to embody the natural response annually in a fast. I call this *body calendar.*

I contend that we need to restore to our spiritual sensibilities that fasting is fundamentally a *response to a grievous sacred moment.* We take on the divine pathos, how God responds to a sacred moment, when we embody our response to those sacred moments in fasting. That is, it is fundamentally an A ➜ B event. Indeed, sometimes (but not always) the A ➜ B response discovers the desired result so that A ➜ B ➜ C occurs. Our contention is that emphasizing B automatically leading to C not only sets up humans for disappointments when things don't work out as desired, but it also creates a new form of legalism and guilt. If one fasts and doesn't get what one wants, then one might be led to question one's motives or one's sanctity. However good it can be to peer into one's motives, the biblical genius for fasting is A prompting B, whether or not C occurs.

Perhaps what we need to become deeper in fasting is bigger eyes and bigger hearts. What we need is greater sensitivity to the plight of others and the grievousness of life's sacred moments. I know scores of folks who are deeply sensitive but do not fast, and I think I know why: our body image. We Westerners have inherited forms of dualism, and the most significant one for spiritual disciplines is the one that teaches that our bodies are not vital for our spirituality. Our discussion of body image sketched a view of our persons that brings the body back into play and advocated that genuine spirituality requires a body-spirit action in which we embody our faith and our hope and our response to God, to ourselves, to others, and to our world.

We are standing today at a fork in the road. We can choose the path that seems as we look into our future to be a path that leads up over some heavy terrain. Or we can choose the easy path, the one that seems to move downward toward a pool of water and into some cool shade. Truth be told, what appears to be the harder path is the path of genuine spirituality, but it means restoring—through some hard work on our part—our bodies to our spirituality.

If we follow the narrower and harder path of integrating body and spirit, we will soon discover ourselves responding to life's grievous moments naturally and inevitably by fasting—not so we can get something. No, instead, we will fast because we will sense God's response to the very conditions around us, and it will lead us to join in the good work of God. I suspect that we will discover that joining God is all we really wanted anyway. I also suspect everything in the desired results column (C) is actually found when we discover we are next to God. Ultimately, then, fasting is being with God and on God's side in the midst of life's grievous sacred moments.

STUDY GUIDE
Fasting
Scot McKnight

"Stand at the crossroads and look; ask for the ancient paths, ask where the good way is, and walk in it, and you will find rest for your souls."
JEREMIAH 6:16

Chapter 1: Fasting and Body Image

Which of the four types of body image (or combination of types) best describes your attitude toward your body?

In what ways do you think changing your body image to one more unified with body and soul would affect your views on fasting and other spiritual disciplines?

PART 1: SPIRITUALITY AND FASTING

Chapter 2: Fasting as Body Talk

Consider for a moment the three types of fasting: the water/juice fast, abstinence, and the absolute fast. Do you ever choose one of these for Lent or other holy day?

Have there been times in your past during which one of these would have been a natural response to a grievous or sacred moment?

Chapter 3: Fasting as Body Turning

In this chapter, the author suggests adding a fast to different moments in our lives: during holy days such as Lent; when God seems absent from us; when we recognize our own complicity in the problems around us; at conversions or baptisms. In what ways could this response to events bind us as a community of faith?

How would fasting at these times deepen our commitment as well as our memories of the events?

Chapter 4: Fasting as Body Plea

How would the addition of fasting to our prayers help unify us, body and spirit, in our pleas to God for help in these five situations?

In what ways do you think fasting could make us more aware of God's guidance and direction than by prayer alone?

Chapter 5: Fasting as Body Grief

Fasting as a natural result of great sorrow is probably the most natural form of fasting. Have you expressed this following a tremendous loss, such as the death of a loved one, a divorce, loss of job or home? In what ways do you think grief and the natural urge to fast show a respect, a way of honoring the depth of that loss?

In what ways does such a fast draw us nearer to God?

Chapter 6: Fasting as Body Discipline

Fasting as a spiritual discipline can easily slip toward a reward-based motive, but as a response to a desire to be closer to God and hold His presence sacred, it has a long history and tradition in the church.

In what ways do you think regular fasts—such as stationary fasts—could prompt deeply spiritual intimacy with God? How could these fasts bring you closer to the unity of your body and mind?

Although such fasts could aid in controlling physical desires, care must be taken that it not become a "body battle." What steps would you need to take to ensure that the fast remains a focused response and not a desire for results?

Chapter 7: Fasting as Body Calendar

Regular, church calendar–based fasts have a long history in our faith. Most come as a response to the sacredness of living a holy life. How would your relationship with God, with those you love, with your fellow believers deepen as a result of regular fasts or observances of holy days, such as Christmas?

The church calendar focuses intently on the life of Jesus. How would participating in regular fasts remind you of his life and love for the church?

Chapter 8: Fasting as Body Poverty

Fasting as a response to local, national, or global issues can bind us as a faith community. What issues of justice or social concern so move you that you could respond with a personal fast? Are there ways this concern could be spread into community solidarity?

Chapter 9: Fasting as Body Contact

This chapter focuses on five great men of the Bible, their fasts, and their intimate encounters with God. If you yearn for a deeper intimacy with God, what can you learn from the stories of these leaders of our faith? How can fasting open your heart, mind, and body to a "more ravishing" worship of our Creator?

Chapter 10: Fasting as Body Hope

Fasting as a response to hope for change is as old as the church itself. In what ways could fasting in hope of real moral, social, and political change intensify your work in the kingdom that is here and hope for the kingdom to come?

What changes could such increased hope make in the way you interact in your civil and faith communities?

PART 2: WISDOM AND FASTING

Chapter 11: Fasting and Its Problems;
Chapter 12: Fasting and Its Benefits

These two chapters take a final look at how fasting can trigger some of the worst human behaviors—and some of the best.

In what way does every problem mentioned in chapter 11 (cheating, hypocrisy, lying, etc.) revert the focus of the fast onto the individual? How can such selfish responses to fasting be best avoided?

How does the natural desire for a "space for God," an intimacy with our Creator, prompt the need to face, to engage our body as well as our spirit in the most vital relationship?

Chapter 13: Fasting and the Body

This chapter focuses on the physiology of fasting; what happens to the body when you fast, both good and bad. Please read it carefully and consult your physician before starting any fast.

ACKNOWLEDGMENTS

WHILE SITTING AT MY DESK ONE DAY IN THE SUMMER OF 2006, I got an e-mail from my friend Phyllis Tickle, who asked if I might be interested in writing a book on fasting in a series on spiritual disciplines. She knew of my interest in the disciplines because of our common interest in fixed-hour prayer, which led to my writing *Praying with the Church*. I want to thank Phyllis for the invitation, and Greg Daniel—then at W Publishing and now my literary agent—for their vision for this series. I am also grateful to Matt Baugher at Thomas Nelson Publishers for his wise, insightful, and helpful advice. Jennifer Stair edited this manuscript carefully and, with delicate care, suggested a major change that made this book better.

Knowing my publication schedule was nearly full when Phyllis called me, I approached Hauna Ondrey, a former student who is now in seminary at North Park Theological Seminary, to see if she would do some library work for me so I could concentrate on the research and writing. Her efforts far exceeded my hopes, and I wish here to record my gratitude. This book would neither be completed nor as good as it is without her insights and suggestions.

I want to thank those who interrupted their schedules to read manuscripts of this book in earlier forms, especially Kent Berghuis, Tracy Balzer, Greg Laughery, and Mindy Caliguire.

In addition, my physician, John Dunlop, MD, helped me with the medical aspects of fasting as did my colleague, Jeff Nelson, MD. Each has made this book better and reminds me again that writing is not a solitary exercise. Writing is participation in the communion of the saints.

Kris, my wife, not only reads all my books but sometimes patiently endures far too many conversations about the books—and she both listens as my mind changes and participates in the conversation in such a way that I must always admit she's partly responsible for everything I write.

Kris and I decided to dedicate this book to two of my former students, who fell in love in one of my classes, who babysat our children as a form of dating, and who now serve St. Matthew's Episcopal in Sterling, Virginia. Thanks, Rob and Linda Merola, for who you are.

RECOMMENDED READING

Akakios, Archimandrite. *Fasting in the Orthodox Church: Its Theological, Pastoral, and Social Implications.* Etna, CA: Center for Traditionalist Orthodox Studies, 1996.

Baab, Lynne M. *Fasting: Spiritual Freedom Beyond Our Appetites.* Downers Grove, IL: InterVarsity, 2006.

Berghuis, Kent. *Christian Fasting: A Theological Approach.* Richardson, TX: Biblical Studies Press, 2007.

de Vogüé, Adalbert. *To Love Fasting: The Monastic Experience*, trans. J. B. Hasbrouck. Petersham, MA: Saint Bede's, 1989.

Foster, Richard. *Celebration of Discipline: The Path to Spiritual Growth*, rev. ed. San Francisco: Harper & Row, 1988.

Grimm, Veronicka. *From Feasting to Fasting, The Evolution of a Sin: Attitudes to Food in Late Antiquity.* New York: Routledge, 1996.

Piper, John. *A Hunger for God: Desiring God through Fasting and Prayer.* Wheaton, IL: Crossway, 1997.

Ryan, Thomas. *The Sacred Art of Fasting: Preparing to Practice.* Woodstock, VT: Skylight Paths, 2005.

Shaw, Teresa. *The Burden of the Flesh: Fasting and Sexuality in Early Christianity.* Minneapolis: Fortress, 1998.

Strack, H. and P. Billerbeck, *Kommentar zum Neuen Testament aus Talmud und Midrasch*, 5 vols. München: C. H. Beck'sche Verlagsbuchhandlung, 1922.

Willard, Dallas. *The Spirit of the Disciplines: Understanding How God Changes Lives.* San Francisco: HarperSanFrancisco, 1988.

NOTES

Introduction: A Montage of Christian Voices on Fasting

1. John Goldingay, *Psalms 1–41* (Grand Rapids: Baker, 2006), 496.
2. Athanasius, "Letter I. Easter, 329," *Nicene and Post-Nicene Fathers*, series 2, vol. 4, trans. A. Robertson (Grand Rapids: Eerdmans, 1978), 507.
3. Augustine, "The Usefulness of Fasting," *The Fathers of the Church* 16, trans. Mary Sarah Muldowney (New York: Fathers of the Church, 1952), 411.
4. John Calvin, *Institutes of the Christian Religion*, Library of Christian Classics (Philadelphia: Westminster, 1975), 2:1242.
5. Andrew Murray, *With Christ in the School of Prayer* (Springdale, PA: Whitaker House, 1981), 101.
6. Adalbert de Vogüé, *To Love Fasting: The Monastic Experience* (Petersham, MA: Saint Bede's Publications, 1989).
7. Dallas Willard, *The Spirit of the Disciplines: Understanding How God Changes Lives* (San Francisco: HarperSanFrancisco, 1991), 111.
8. John Piper, *A Hunger for God: Desiring God through Fasting and Prayer* (Wheaton, IL: Crossway, 1997), 104.
9. Thomas Ryan, *The Sacred Art of Fasting: Preparing to Practice* (Woodstock, VT: SkyLight Paths, 2006), 40.
10. Amy Johnson Frykholm, "Soul Food: Why Fasting Makes Sense," *Christian Century* (March 8, 2005), 24.

Chapter 1: Fasting and Body Image

1. Thomas Howard, *The Night Is Far Spent: A Treasury of Thomas Howard*, selected by Vivian W. Dudro (San Francisco: Ignatius, 2007), 62.
2. Still the best study of the anthropology of the Old Testament is that of Hans Walter Wolff, *Anthropology of the Old Testament*, trans. M. Kohl (Philadelphia: Fortress, 1974).
3. Frederica Mathewes-Green, "To Hell on a Cream Puff," *Christianity Today* (November 13, 1999), 44.
4. John Paul II, *Man and Woman He Created Them: A Theology of the Body*, trans. M. Waldstein (Boston: Pauline Books and Media, 2006).

5. Another important study along this line is F. LeRon Shults, *Reforming Theological Anthropology: After the Philosophical Turn to Relationality* (Grand Rapids: Eerdmans, 2003).
6. Kathleen Dugan, "Fasting for Life: The Place of Fasting in the Christian Tradition," *Journal of the American Academy of Religion* 63 (1995): 548.

Chapter 2: Fasting as Body Talk

1. For a good survey of the theories of human nature, see Leslie Stevenson, David L. Haberman, *Ten Theories of Human Nature*, 4th ed. (New York: Oxford, 2004).
2. Philosophers sometimes call body and spirit and soul and conscience "moments" of the person. Body or spirit or soul or conscience are not "parts" of the person, but "moments" of—dimensions of experiencing—the person. Whether we call it "inner and outer" or "moments of the person," the point we need to make is this: God designed us as unified persons who are embodied.
3. Lynne M. Baab, *Fasting: Spiritual Freedom Beyond Our Appetites* (Downers Grove, IL: InterVarsity Press, 2006), 71.

Chapter 3: Fasting as Body Turning

1. Andrew Greeley, Michael Hout, *The Truth about Conservative Christians* (Chicago: University of Chicago, 2006), 103–12.

Chapter 4: Fasting as Body Plea

1. Azar Nafisi, *Reading Lolita in Tehran* (New York: Random House, 2003); Alan Paton, *Cry, the Beloved Country* (New York: Scribner, 2003).
2. See 2 Chronicles 20:3; Nehemiah 9:1; Esther 4:3, 16; and Luke 2:37.
3. Pete Greig, *God on Mute: Engaging the Silence of Unanswered Prayer* (Ventura, CA: Regal, 2007), "About the Author."
4. Ibid., 32–33.

Chapter 6: Fasting as Body Discipline

1. Adalbert de Vogüé, *To Love Fasting: The Monastic Experience* (Petersham, MA: Saint Bede's Publications, 1989).
2. Ibid., 6.
3. Ibid., 8, 9, 10.
4. Ibid., 15.
5. Dallas Willard, *The Spirit of the Disciplines: Understanding How God Changes Lives* (San Francisco: HarperSanFrancisco, 1988), 95–129.
6. Ibid., 99.
7. If interested, two good sources are Stephen G. Miller, *Ancient Greek Athletics* (New Haven: Yale University Press, 2004); Michael B. Poliakoff,

Combat Sports in the Ancient World: Competition, Violence, and Culture (New Haven: Yale University Press, 1987). Though not as central to culture, sports interested Jews as well: the only book I know of on this topic is H. A. Harris, *Greek Athletics and the Jews* (Cardiff: University of Wales Press, 1976).

8. There are exceptional studies of the early church, the body, sexuality, and fasting: see especially Veronicka Grimm, *From Feasting to Fasting, The Evolution of a Sin: Attitudes to Food in Late Antiquity* (London: Routledge, 1996); and Teresa Shaw, *The Burden of the Flesh: Fasting and Sexuality in Early Christianity* (Minneapolis: Fortress, 1998); see also V. L. Wimbush, ed., *Ascetic Behavior in Greco-Roman Antiquity: A Sourcebook* (Minneapolis: Fortress, 1990). More wide-ranging is Peter Brown, *The Body and Society: Men, Women, and Sexual Renunciation in Early Christianity* (New York: Columbia University Press, 1988).

9. de Vogüé, *To Love Fasting*, 33.

10. Arthur Wallis, *God's Chosen Fast: A Spiritual and Practical Guide to Fasting* (Fort Washington, PA: Christian Literature Crusade, 1997), 92.

11. Jerome, *Life of Paul, the First Hermit*, 6. Quoted in Veronica Grimm, *From Feasting to Fasting*, 160.

12. Jerome, *Letters* 45.3. Quoted in Veronicka Grimm, *From Feasting to Fasting*, 164; emphasis added. On Jerome, see J. N. D. Kelly, *Jerome: His Life, Writings, and Controversies* (Peabody, MA: Hendrickson, 2000), 179–94.

13. Mohandas K. Gandhi, *Gandhi An Autobiography: The Story of My Experiments with Truth*, trans. M. Desai (Boston: Beacon, 1993), 332.

14. Athanasius, *The Life of St. Anthony*, trans. R. T. Meyer (Westminster, MD: New Press, 1950). Quotations, in order of appearance, are from sections 7, 14, 45, 93. In spite of the centuries-long popularity of Anthony's life, I confess to finding his asceticism extreme.

Chapter 7: Fasting as Body Calendar

1. John Wesley, *Works of John Wesley* (Grand Rapids: Zondervan, 1958), 4.94.

2. Ibid.

3. For a brief detailing of the early history of the church calendar, see John F. Baldovin, "The Empire Baptized," in *The Oxford History of Christian Worship*, ed. Geoffrey Wainwright, Karen B. Westerfield Tucker (New York: Oxford, 2006), 112–20.

4. Robert Webber, *Ancient-Future Worship: Proclaiming and Enacting God's Narrative* (Grand Rapids: Baker, 2008), 29.

5. Scot McKnight, *Praying with the Church* (Brewster, MA: Paraclete Press, 2006).

6. *Institutes of John Cassian*, 5.20. Nicene and Post-Nicene Fathers, series 2, vol. 11, trans. Edgar C. S. Gibson (Grand Rapids: Eerdmans, 1986).

7. "The Canonical Epistle," from The Ante-Nicene Fathers, vol. 6, trans. James B. H. Hawkins (Grand Rapids: Eerdmans, 1971).

8. Wesley, *Works of John Wesley*, 19.88.

9. *Constitutions of the Holy Apostles*, Ante-Nicene Fathers, vol. 7, trans. William Whiston, ed. James Donaldson (Grand Rapids: Eerdmans, 1975), 7.2.23.

10. Tertullian, "*The Chaplet, or De Corona*," Ante-Nicene Fathers, vol. 3, trans. S. Thelwall (Grand Rapids: Eerdmans, 1980), 3.

11. Jerome, *Letters* 71 (to Lucinius), Nicene and Post-Nicene Fathers, series 2, vol. 6, trans. W. H. Fremantle (Grand Rapids: Eerdmans, 1989), 6.

12. *Constitutions of the Holy Apostles*, 8.47.64.

13. *The Council of Gangra*, Nicene and Post-Nicene Fathers, series 2, vol. 14, trans. Henry R. Percival (Grand Rapids: Eerdmans, 1971), canon 18.

14. *Letters of St. Augustine*, 54.7.9. Nicene and Post-Nicene Fathers, series 1, vol. 1 (Grand Rapids: Eerdmans, 1988). The translation is that of J. G. Cunningham.

15. Wesley, *Works of John Wesley*, 4.95.

16. *Recognitions of Clement*, 7.34. Ante-Nicene Fathers 8 (Grand Rapids: Eerdmans, 1974). The translation is that of Thomas Smith.

17. *Letters of Athanasius*, 6. Nicene and Post-Nicene Fathers, series 2, vol. 4, trans. A. Robertson (Grand Rapids: Eerdmans, 1978), 6; emphasis added.

18. Augustine, *Homilies on the Gospel of John*, Nicene and Post-Nicene Fathers, series 1, vol. 7, trans. John Gibb and James Innes (Grand Rapids: Eerdmans, 1956), 17.4.

19. A very good book on this is by Archimandrite Akakios, *Fasting in the Orthodox Church: Its Theological, Pastoral, and Social Implications* (Etna, CA: Center for Traditionalist Orthodox Studies, 1996). Orthodoxy's rich resource for spirituality, with an abundance of charming stories and personal examples that in many ways rival the Talmuds of Judaism, is *The Philokalia: The Complete Text*, 4 vols. (London: Faber and Faber, 1983), and fasting can be accessed by using the indices.

20. Ember days refer to four sets of three days in the church calendar that were set apart for fasting and prayer, and Rogation Days refer to the Monday–Wednesday before Ascension Day (a Thursday).

21. Martin Luther, *Luther's Works*, vol. 21: *The Sermon on the Mount* (St. Louis, MO: Concordia, 1956), 159.

Chapter 8: Fasting as Body Poverty

1. I borrow this expression from Tom Holmén, *Jesus and Jewish Covenant Thinking* (Leiden: E. J. Brill, 2001).

2. Abraham Heschel, *The Prophets*, 2 vols. (New York: Harper Torchbooks, 1969). The theme is found throughout the two volumes.

3. On Isaiah, I refer always to H. G. M. Williamson, *Variations on a Theme: King, Messiah and Servant in the Book of Isaiah* (London: Paternoster, 1988).

4. The Shepherd of Hermas 56:3. Loeb Classical Library, trans. Bart Ehrman (Cambridge, MA: Harvard, 2005), 25.

5. Augustine, *Expositions on the Book of Psalms*, 43.7. Nicene and Post-Nicene Fathers, series 1, vol. 8 (Grand Rapids: Eerdmans, 1974). The translation is called the Oxford translation and is only slightly edited by A. Cleveland Coxe.

6. Wesley, *Works of John Wesley*, 20.10.

7. For a social-science perspective on fasting, see B. J. Malina, *Christian Origins and Cultural Anthropology: Practical Models for Biblical Interpretation* (Atlanta: John Knox Press, 1986), 185–204.

8. "The Congressman Who Can't Stomach Hunger," *Christianity Today* (June 20, 1994), 15.

9. Ibid., 17.

10. See David Duncombe, "Prayer and Fasting in the Halls of Congress: A Pastoral Approach to Lobbying," *Journal of Pastoral Care* 55 (2001): 7–16. All quotations from his life are from this article.

11. See http://www.jubileeresearch.org/jubilee2000/news/usa1709.html.

12. Eamon Duffy, "To Fast Again," *First Things* 151 (2005): 5.

13. St. Chrysostom, *Concerning the Statues*, 3.11–2; 16.13. Nicene and Post-Nicene Fathers, series 1, vol. 9 (Grand Rapids: Eerdmans, 1989). The translation is that of W .R. W. Stephens, though I have updated slightly.

14. Lynne M. Baab, *Fasting: Spiritual Freedom Beyond Our Appetites* (Downers Grove, IL: InterVarsity, 2006), 16.

Chapter 9: Fasting as Body Contact

1. Phillip H. Wiebe, *Visions of Jesus: Direct Encounters from the New Testament to Today* (New York: Oxford University Press, 1997).

2. John Cassian, *Institutes* 22; *First Conference of Abbot Moses*, 7, 8.

3. Nahum Sarna, *Exodus*, JPS Torah Commentary (Philadelphia: JPS, 1991), 220.

4. Athanasius, "Letter 1, Easter 329," 6. Nicene and Post-Nicene Fathers, series 2, vol. 4, (Grand Rapids: Eerdmans, 1978), trans. A. Robertson.

5. Basil the Great, "Letters," 45.1. Nicene and Post-Nicene Fathers, series 2, vol. 8; trans. Blomfield Jackson (Grand Rapids: Eerdmans, n.d.).

6. John Calvin, *Institutes of the Christian Religion* (Library of Christian Classics; Philadelphia: Westminster, 1975), 2.1242.

Chapter 10: Fasting as Body Hope

1. I am grateful to Kent Berghuis for an electronic version of his PhD dissertation, which is now in print as *Christian Fasting: A Theological Approach* (Biblical Studies Press, 2007).

2. I have focused here on Luke's presentation of this passage. Both Mark and Matthew give a slightly different image for the parable of the torn cloth. Mark 2:21 says "otherwise, the patch pulls away from it, the new from the old, and a worse tear is made." Matthew agrees with Mark—suggesting the image is about a patch of unshrunk cloth tearing an older garment when the patch shrinks through washing and drying and aging. I believe the ending of Luke's passage should be read with a mischievous smile on Jesus' part, and is almost certainly not part of the parable: "And no one after drinking old wine desires new wine, but says 'The old is good.'" This is humorous, not a comment on the inadequacy of the new wine Jesus brings (and is!).

3. Thomas Ryan, *The Sacred Art of Fasting: Preparing to Practice* (Woodstock, VT: SkyLight Paths, 2006), 39.

4. A Monk of the Eastern Church, *Orthodox Spirituality*, 2d ed. (Crestwood, NY: St. Vladimir's Seminary Press, 1996), 22.

5. Bradley Nassif, private e-mail correspondence, April 2, 2008.

6. Kent Berghuis, "Christian Fasting: A Theological Approach," (PhD dissertation, (Trinity Evangelical Divinity School, 2002), 163.

Chapter 11: Fasting and Its Problems

1. Luther, *Luther's Works*, 21, 157

2. Ibid., 158. John Calvin confirms this problem in *Institutes*, 4.12.21.

3. Basil's sermon *About Fasting* 1, 31.184 [10].

4. Jerome, "Letters of St. Jerome," Nicene and Post-Nicene Fathers, series 2, vol. 6, trans. W. H. Fremantle, G. Lewis, and W. G. Martley (Grand Rapids: Eerdmans, 1989), letter 22.37.

5. St. Chrysostom, "The Gospel of Matthew." Nicene and Post-Nicene Fathers, series, vol. 10, trans. G. Prevost (Grand Rapids: Eerdmans, 1986), 30.4.

6. Ibid., 25.3. I have slightly edited the translation to make it more readable.

7. Etan Levine contends that the disfiguring of the face in fasting was a reference to the use of wood ashes from the Torah ark, and it evoked the sufficiency of Isaac's offering of himself on the altar as atonement for sins. Hence, the disfiguring refers to the sprinkling of Isaac's ashes for atonement. Since Jesus did not believe in that kind of atonement, but only in that of his own death, the denial of disfiguring is a statement about atonement. This study can be found at *Journal of Ritual Studies* 13.1 (1999): 106. I have my doubts because the context of Matthew 6:1-18 favors a concern more with ostentatiousness than with atonement. It is true, as Levine observes, that Jesus did not prohibit sackcloth, etc., but only disfiguring the face.

8. Luther, *Luther's Works* 21, 158.

9. Jerome, "Letters of St. Jerome," letter 22.7.

10. John Cassian, "Second Conference of Abbot Moses," 17.
11. Jerome, "Letters of St. Jerome," letter 107.10.
12. Ibid., letter 130.17.
13. St. Chrysostom, "Concerning the Statues," Nicene and Post-Nicene Fathers, series 2, vol. 9, trans. W. R. Stephens (Grand Rapids: Eerdmans, 1989), homily 15.1.

Chapter 12: Fasting and Its Benefits

1. John Piper, *A Hunger for God: Desiring God Through Fasting and Prayer* (Wheaton, IL: Crossway, 1997), 67–68.
2. Basil's sermon, *About Fasting*, translated in K. Berghuis, *Christian Fasting*, 188, (31.172 [6]).
3. *Confessions* (trans. P. Burton; New York: A. A. Knopf, 2001), 1.1.1.
4. Ibid.
5. Wesley, *Works of John Wesley*, 5.441.
6. Piper, *A Hunger for God*, 14.
7. Willard, *The Spirit of the Disciplines*.
8. Richard Foster, *Celebration of Discipline: The Path to Spiritual Growth*, rev. ed. (San Francisco: Harper & Row, 1988), 55.

Chapter 13: Fasting and the Body

1. I won't give the names of medical doctors and nurses to whom I have spoken about fasting, but I draw attention to two sources that have been helpful: Lee Goldman and Dennis Ausiello, eds., *Cecil Textbook of Medicine*, 22d ed. (Philadelphia Saunders, 2004); Jerrold B. Leikin and Martin S. Lipsky, eds., *American Medical Association Complete Medical Encyclopedia* (New York: Random House Reference, 2003).
2. I rely here especially on Teresa Shaw, *The Burden of the Flesh*, chapter 2.
3. Wesley, *Works of John Wesley*, 18, 123.
4. *Cecil Textbook of Medicine*, s.v. "Metabolic Response to Starvation," 1317.

ABOUT THE AUTHOR

Scot McKnight is an Anabaptist theologian and the Karl A. Olsson Professor in Religious Studies at North Park University (Chicago, Illinois). The author of more than twenty books, including *The Jesus Creed*, McKnight specializes in Jesus studies and the New Testament. McKnight, a Beliefnet.com blogger, has been frequently consulted by news media throughout the United States. He and his wife, Kristen, live in Libertyville, Illinois. They have two adult children, Laura and Lukas.

THE ANCIENT PRACTICES SERIES

PHYLLIS TICKLE, GENERAL EDITOR

Stand at the crossroads and look; ask for the ancient paths,
ask where the good way is, and walk in it,
and you will find rest for your souls.

—JEREMIAH 6:16 NIV

THOMAS NELSON
Since 1798